The
BLUES
ALIVE

The
BLUES
ALIVE

The Timeless Tradition

Ed Flaherty
of SHRI

Hohm Press
Prescott, Arizona
1999

Layout and Design: Mel Lions; Jaye Pratt at AlphaCat Design

Cover: Kim Johansen

First Printing: March 1998

ISBN: 0-934252-86-6

Library of Congress: 98-071634

Hohm Press
PO Box 2501
Prescott, AZ 86302
1-800-381-2700
http://www.booknotes.com/hohm/pinedr@goodnet.com

Photo Acknowledgements:
Pg. 62, pg. 70, pg. 96, from: *The Land Where the Blues Began* by Allan Lomax.
Copyright © 1993 by Alan Lomax, reprinted by permission of Pantheon
Books, a division of Random House, Inc.

About the Typeface

This book was set in Centaur, a typface designed by the American
typographer Bruce Rogers in 1929. Centaur was a typeface which
Rogers adapted from the fifteenth-century type of Nicolas Jenson
and modified in 1948 for a cutting by the Monotype Corporation.

*To all the blues masters, past and present, whose beautiful
generosity of spirit has preserved this priceless lineage.*

Acknowledgments

Thanks to all who those have enthusiastically participated in and supported Shri—past, present and future. You have shown how much can be accomplished when we all come together to manifest our vision:

Lee Lozowick, for his radiant inspiration, brilliant humor and his willingness to put his body on the line one hundred percent. And for teaching us the essence of the blues.

Deborah Auletta, for her constant warm support and encouragement, her incredible meals and big hearted generosity. Oh yeah, and she's one hell of a singer.

Shukyo Lin Rainey, for her beautiful passion and zest for life, and for the incredible energy she put into the project. We all wish her the best.

Tina Zuccarello, for her amazing ability to accept all our quirks and her total belief in and commitment to Shri. And for her wonderful smile.

Heather Chinery, for the tireless devotion she has exhibited in becoming our newest member.

Regina Sara Ryan, my editor of great faith, who sang background harmonies at the first ever Shri gig (put that on your resume!).

Karuna Fedorshak and Kelsey Bogart, for putting their hearts into it in the crucial early days of the band.

e.e., for her loyal devotion and service (thanks for postering!), and her panache.

Bill Augood, for getting the job done no matter what, and with good humor as well.

Matthew Files, our loyal soundman, for his unconventional humor and his significant silences.

Zachary Parker, who helped us through our first tour of France with grace and good spirits.

Jim Capellini, who has preached our message far and wide and supported us beyond the call of duty.

Doug Fulker, who helped get the band rolling and has graced our stage many times with his playful presence.

Stan Hitson, (a true gentleman if ever there was one) for his invaluable help, especially in the studio.

George Nardo, not only a one-of-a-kind engineer and producer, but an outstanding human being.

All the rest of liars, gods and beggars—Steve Ball, Justin Hitson, Everett Jaime, Dan Fitz and Peter Cohen—who have generously supported us onstage and off.

Nachama Greenwald and Denise Cavitt, whose unbridled enthusiasm is bringing fresh energy to the band.

Sylvan Incao, for providing superlative help at the last minute.

For all the others who have traveled with us on the road and come to our gigs over the years—you don't know just how much we appreciate your support.

My parents for all their love and support, and for buying me my first electric guitar—a good gift choice.

Contents

Introduction

"This is the last generation of old-time blues players. When they go, that's it." I let the weight of the words sink in, momentarily stunned by the possibility of this loss. I did not want to believe it. For the past several years I had been seeking out obscure recordings and books, mining the rich vein of blues lore, obsessed with exploring what it was about the blues that was gripping my heart, stirring up too long ignored feelings of longing and bringing me into deeper contact with myself and with life.

I had just met Ken, a fellow blues lover and concert promoter who had also played keyboard with some of the greats. We were sitting in the cafeteria of the Peer R&B Festival, one of Europe's premier blues events. The café was a huge tent bustling with musicians, promoters and festival volunteers. A P.A. system piped in music from the show, and a large array of video monitors captured the action onstage from every direction. Outside, rain fell persistently, turning the festival grounds into a giant mudbath. I asked Ken: "But don't you think that what was real in that music is being passed down?"

As Ken was thinking over the question, I could hear the approaching din of drums and horns. It was the St. Gabriel's Celestial New Orleans Brass Band, a dozen black men who marched around the muddy fields between every set to give us a taste of their raucous, old-time jazz. These mischievous pied pipers marched right into the place as if they owned it. They all wore loud red, white and blue jackets, emblazoned on the back with a picture of Uncle Sam wearing sunglasses, over which was the insignia, "Ambassadors of American Culture." A sly joke. Their wiry leader commanded the space with his shrill whistle and gnarled wooden baton with an almost demonic intensity. He stopped in the middle of the crowd as the band snaked around him. A wild dance erupted straight out of the earth through his feet and into his pelvis, crazy contortions sending important messages throughout the room. Snare drums cracked and rattled our brains. Bass drums boomed deep in our bodies, trumpets whined, saxophones wailed, trombones growled—like a conversation where everyone talks at once, loudly. They were mixing up a devilish stew of sound, a barely contained vortex of chaos, inciting the crowd into a jubilant frenzy. The sound seemed intent on wiping the mind clean of all rational thought. I fought my impulse to get up and shout and join the fray, wanting to continue the conversation.

Ken went on: "I don't think it can be passed down. The culture that created this music is gone. Segregation created a kind of isolation. All the pain and suffering of the black people had nowhere to go except into the music—blues and jazz. Oh yeah, and the church of course, and from there came more music, gospel and soul. But now the whole thing's been opened up. They say that communication destroys culture. When this generation goes, the loss will be irreversible."

It was true that that world was gone. I thought of those scratchy old recordings, wails and moans of a bottleneck caressing the strings of an old beat-up guitar, conveying all the longing and anguish I had ever felt, but could not express. The blues somehow gave me back a piece of my soul I didn't even know I had lost. But, even though Ken's viewpoint made rational sense, I couldn't accept it. Something inside me cried, "No!" For me, the blues was as alive as ever, alive because I felt them too. I needed to pursue this trail to the end, to capture the secret of this elusive feeling, to find the source of this s.o.s. that washed up on the shore of my soul. The music was a thread leading to something real, something that was definitely missing from my life, as well as from the culture at large. It was sung by those who had tasted life directly and knew the visceral truths that are so often ignored today. When nothing else seemed to address these truths, the blues came along and told me about longing and heartache, erotic play and celebration of life.

I kept prodding Ken: "But don't you think today's blues is just as real? Things may be different, but it still comes from the soul." Ken nodded, but didn't say anything. I was left with this question churning inside me. I knew the answer was a matter of my own experience. "The blues is a feeling," goes the time-worn adage, and I was going to have to dig deeper to find it.

Finding My Soulmates

Five years ago, before I joined Shri, these questions and feelings were a jumbled-up mess of inchoate longing without a means of expression. I had actually just sold my guitar and amp because I couldn't find anyone in my town that I wanted to play with. Then Shri popped up out of nowhere—I saw them play at a friend's party, five women stumbling along on their instruments and having a damn good time doing it. They had a warm inviting presence that put people at ease, and it looked like with a little more confidence they could incite a small riot. And I liked that the keyboardist, Kelsey (who is no longer with us), used her ironing board for a keyboard stand, and that Deborah kicked off her shoes to sing in her bare feet (a mode of dress she still prefers)—no pretension in this band.

Deborah on lead vocals exuded a natural power and presence which made her the obvious choice for the frontperson. One of the cover songs she picked that day—the classic, *You Can Have My Husband*

(*But Please Don't Mess With My Man*)—showed off her irrepressible good humor and panache. Shukyo on drums (also no longer with us) played with enough energy and enthusiasm for two bands, and cool Tina was all smiles as usual playing her shiny new electric bass.

Months earlier, Tina and Deborah had gotten together on a lark to play a few old-time songs, with funky titles like *Nail That Catfish to the Tree*. At the time, Tina was playing a stand up bass which was as tall as she was, and had to augment her 5 foot 3 inches by standing on several phone books. They had no idea that their little hobby would eventually take over their lives, bringing them to every little podunk town in Arizona you could think of (with picturesque names like Cornville), as well as the big concert stages of Europe.

I had heard through a mutual friend that they were looking for a lead guitarist, and something inside me jumped on the opportunity before my mind could say, "You're crazy!" I had just sold all my equipment, but luckily the person I sold it to wanted to sell it back. I was back in business. Shri was now an *almost* all women's blues band. However, there was one troubling condition for my joining the band....

The First Gig

It was a sweltering July afternoon in Prescott, Arizona. We were set up under a large wooden gazebo, near the Granite Dells, a two billion year old deposit of huge granite boulders seemingly strewn around a silent lake. The stark, timeless beauty of this place was like nothing I'd ever seen. Dark pools of water lay silent and still like black glass. The ominous boulders, standing like sentinels, throw light and shadow, creating an eerie other-worldly landscape. As the sun sets, a blanket of color—muted hues of orange and red, purple and pink—descends on this scene, illuminating the rocks with a warm glow, as if their heat is radiating out from the inside.

Unfortunately, the scenery was lost on me this day. My first time out on stage with my new bandmates I was a nervous wreck. My guitar, which my parents had given me for my birthday ten years before, hung like an lead weight around my neck. My new black and white jumper (which I had bought from our drummer's daughter) was clinging to my sticky body uncomfortably, and the skirt was embarrassingly short. No matter how much help I got from the women, *no force on earth could get my hair right.* I was sure my makeup was smeared all over my face from the unbearable heat. And no sooner would I return from the toilet than I would have to go again with even more urgency. To top it all off, there was a brick in my stomach where the undigested barbecue chicken I just ate lay in wait to ruin my brand new dress.

"How do these women do this?" I thought. "How do they spend so much time, attention and energy on how they look, and then walk down the street like nothing was wrong? This is hell." Needless to say, my first experience wearing a dress in public was not easy, especially coupled with the nervousness one always feels before going onstage for the first time with a new group. Is this why they wanted (no, forced!) me to wear a dress: so I would know what it was like to be a woman? To make a statement of solidarity? It was my initiation into another world. I was a sister now, part of the All Women's Blues Band: Shri. I felt like shouting, "I'm a woman and I'm proud!" (But I was too close to throwing up.) That gig was my first and last in drag. I had passed the test. And I did manage to fool a few people. Despite my 6 feet 2 inches, my gangly limbs and my impossible hair, I somehow fit in (I have to say I got plenty of compliments on my legs though—I guess that skirt worked after all!)

I had played with a lot of other musicians in this town, but nothing ever clicked. No soul, no chemistry, no alchemy, heat, magic, whatever. They may have had the chops, but there was something else missing. The notes may have been right, but where was the heart behind the notes? Where was the person who had something to say, something to give, who gave *into* the feeling? I didn't know it at the time, but I was looking for something more than simply making good music; I was looking for a personal connection with other musicians that could create something special.

I had finally found them in Shri, musicians who put being a genuine person before being a musician with all the "chops." That first gig was a celebration, a homecoming, a recognition that we were all following the same path, using music (or letting music use us) to get to something real inside ourselves, to overcome our fears and allow ourselves to be vulnerable. Our audience felt it too and gave that feeling back to us in turn. The almost unanimous response that day was one of shocked delight. One of our friends was so moved by the reality of an (almost) all women's blues band, she actually broke into tears the first several times she heard us play. Maybe it had something to do with the meaning of "Shri"—the secret in the heart of a woman.

That afternoon, we played our eleven-song set list with total abandon, and one punk/blues number we did actually incited some playful slam dancing. Despite the fact that the beginnings and endings of songs would mysteriously inflict either paralytic conditions or uncontrollable spasms upon most of us, one thing was obvious on that first day: this band had a chemistry that was fresh and enticing. We began a love affair with our audiences that has continued to grow and deepen over the last five years.

All of our gigs are a chance to let ourselves go, to be swept away by something bigger than ourselves, and to communicate with the audience and each other from a real place inside ourselves. The magic of music is that somehow it makes being onstage a safe place to be vulnerable. But it's not just any music—for us, it's the blues that provides the text and hymns for our service. The blues is the vehicle which allows us to work ourselves into a kind of controlled frenzy where improvisational passion and conviction of feeling blend together. Then we take that blues bible and whomp people over the head with it (in a nice way, of course). Yes, we're serious about our music: it's the Church of the Blues—to sing is to testify, to bend that guitar string is to confess the truth.

After some time, I figured out what it was about Shri that attracted me: for them, music was about love—feeling it, communicating it. That's what had been missing for me all those years. When it comes to playing the blues, our blues, we have been amazed time and time again at the power of music to heal our wounds and open up the door to friendship, gratitude and love. We feel it, and the audience feels it too.

We had all found a kind of sanctuary with each other in playing the blues. I had always liked the blues, but it wasn't until I really got into playing them that I understood their appeal. For me, the blues opened up a new way of expression, a way of concentrating on what I felt inside instead of what note I was going to play next. It was revolutionary. I had never realized how much my mind was getting in the way of simply enjoying music. Years before, I had scorned "three chord songs" as somehow being beneath me, too simple to count as real music. Now my attitude has changed dramatically, although the three chord formation is still not my favorite—I'll take a one chord song over that any day.

The more we played, the more we wanted to play. The music was taking us to forgotten places inside: deserted side streets of the soul; ancient burial sites of lost loves; hidden rivers of the heart. Each gig was an opportunity to mine for gold, to go a little deeper inside than we had gone before. The blues was a doorway to discovering a whole other side to myself, the side of feeling, intuition and passion. I had been knocking on the door to my heart to no avail, until I found that playing music with Shri was the key I was missing.

That realization was the seed for this book. The more I learned about the history of the blues and the more music I heard, the more I could feel the profound gift that African American culture has given to all of us. (I found out that it was not simply that we happened to like the music, found it catchy and upbeat. That couldn't explain the huge impact that jazz, blues and gospel music have had this century). In fact what is known as American music is to a large degree African American music; it is so much a part of our culture, that we completely take it for granted. America *desperately* needed something that the blues happened to provide. This book is an attempt to explain exactly what it was that American society was missing and how the blues answered this need.

A book of this nature could look more closely at jazz and gospel to give a more complete picture of the African American contribution, but I see that as a much larger project somewhere down the road. Although we will cover a lot of historical and factual data, this book is not essentially a scholarly endeavor—it is about my personal experiences playing the blues with Shri. This band has taught me a lot more about the blues than scores of books and old recordings could ever teach me. The blues can only be lived, never imitated. What is living the blues? The best answer I can come up with is this: the complete acceptance of all that life has to offer, saying 'yes' to life so profoundly that it breaks one's heart.

All of us in Shri (Deborah our vocalist; Tina on bass; Heather on drums; me on guitar; together with Matthew, our loyal sound man and Lee our wild lyricist) have known these blues intimately from time to time in our travels together. It is not easy keeping six individuals with different needs and opinions all going in the same direc-

Shri's latest incarnation: (top, left to right) Heather Chinery, Ed Flaherty; (bottom, left to right) Tina Zuccarello, Deborah Auletta.

tion. There are many moments of joy and closeness between us, but there are at least an equal number of times of despair, times when I feel totally alone and powerless to change others or myself; when I lose all faith in myself and my friends and the possibility of reconciliation; or worst of all, when I can find no solace in the music and I've seemingly lost the key to my own heart. Sometimes it just closes down. Sometimes others' hearts do too. That is when we need the blues the most. If we can sing or play what we feel at that moment, in our blackest despair, we have found a kind of healing, a home in the blues, because the blues takes in lost souls, those that have no other place to go.

The Oldest Story

Sadness and happiness would well up in me with the first few notes. Why is it I said to myself, that listening to this music I feel a homesickness for a vanished world I was never a part of.
—Charles Simic[1]

Homesickness is as good a word as any to describe the human condition as it shows up in late twentieth century America. We are a restless nation, a people without roots—geographically, communally, spiritually; and we are paying the price. A deep anxiety about God-knows-what grips the country. Just listen to talk radio for a week.

Where I live, a small city in Arizona, I am actually surprised when I meet someone who was born here. Everyone is from somewhere else. The average American moves once every five years, and some much more frequently than that. Are we all looking for a "vanished world?"

I think we are searching for a sense of community, culture and tradition that was lost as dozens of different ethnic groups came overseas, changed their names, dropped their accents and cultural idiosyncrasies as fast as they could, and attempted to become their idea of an American. If this country was ever truly a melting pot, it only succeeded in boiling out all the uniqueness of the rich cultures that originally jumped in the soup, leaving only limp overcooked vegetables devoid of taste and nutrients. For instance, where I grew up in New York City in the 1970s, there were still vestiges of the old neighborhood mentality with groups of Irish, Italians, Germans, Puerto Ricans, Jews and Hungarians retaining strong ethnic flavors. Now, twenty years later, my old neighborhood has been invaded by dozens of towering condominium complexes. The old neighborhoods are disappearing. I fear that everyone is becoming the same.

Alan Lomax wrote about the uncanny precognition the blues had in recognizing these widespread social problems. His book, *The Land Where the Blues Began*, documents the lives of poor sharecroppers and musicians with uncommon honesty, compassion and unsentimentality, all the while providing insightful scholarship:

> . . . all of us are beginning to experience the melancholy dissatisfaction that weighed upon the hearts of the Mississippi Delta, the land where the blues began. Feelings of anomie and alienation, of orphaning and rootlessness—the sense of being a commodity rather than a person; the loss of love and family and place—this modern syndrome was the norm for the cotton farmers and the transient laborers of the Deep South a hundred years ago.[2]

Lomax called the twentieth century the "century of the blues," because of how perfectly these lonely and hopeless blues songs capture the prevailing mood of the times.

As Americans, being uprooted is in our blood. Our first ancestors, the Puritans, left their home to escape religious tyranny, endur-

2

ing a treacherous sea voyage, starvation and attacks by Indians. Stirred by their example, more and more Europeans risked death to start a new life on this soil. Let's face it: America was founded and populated by displaced persons who, for one reason or another, couldn't make it in their own land. We are a nation of outcasts.

And still, many immigrants didn't settle down on the east coast, but kept pushing out further and further west to stake their claim, find their spot in the sun. As they spread out across the continent, hundreds of Indian nations were laid waste, and those few remaining were forced onto desolate reservations. More displaced peoples.

California was the ultimate goal—the westernmost shore (has a mystical ring to it, doesn't it?). From the 1850s until fairly recently, Americans flocked to the place that was supposed to be *it*. But overpopulation, crime, pollution, suburban wastelands and natural disasters have turned California, our dream of paradise, into a painful reality. Now, even the Californians are moving on. During one year alone, several thousand migrated to my little Arizona hideaway, and we now have more espresso bars than we know what to do with. Everyone is searching for the perfect little town where one can settle down and raise a family in peace and quiet. But once people find out about one of these places, it's never too long before they're overrun by unhappy city dwellers or suburbanites. Pretty soon the crime rate is going up and there's a drug problem in the schools. Instead of confronting the reality of our lives, we are much more likely to move onto the next "perfect little hometown."*

Of course, the African Americans who spawned the blues were well acquainted with homesickness. They felt it in their bones, for

*In fact, the Disney Corporation has designed such a place in Florida—the first corporate township complete with Disney logos on the manhole covers (this is not a joke). Disney Inc., the master creators of fantasy, is now creating "reality" for those who are longing for a "hometown" like they grew up in, or even one that they imagined their parents grew up in.

they and their ancestors did not choose to come here. Whole families and tribes were shipped across the sea in the greatest forced migration history has ever known. And it didn't end there. Once in the South, they could be traded and moved like so much cattle, with little regard for the sacredness of communal or family ties. Even after slavery's end, blacks had little security, and many were forced to wander about for their livelihood, sometimes from the age of ten.

Uprooted from their ancient tribal homeland in Africa and faced with bleak opportunities everywhere they looked, most African Americans became inured to a desolate life of wandering. Religion (either Jesus or Hoodoo) and music became their protection and solace from succumbing to the horrendous abuse that blacks on the road in America were forced to endure. No wonder this feeling of homesickness wells up in the blues and tinges each note with longing and heartbreak—it was built into the African American culture. They were a people who had lost their way and come asunder.

> Well if I feel tomorrow
> Like I feel today
> I'm gonna pack my suitcase
> And make my getaway
> I be's troubled. I'm all worried in mind
> And I never be satisfied
> And I just can't keep from cryin'.
> —Muddy Waters[3]

Laying Down Our Burden

The power of the blues is in this: we are never just listening to one person's tale of hardship, no matter how personal the story; every song is a tap into a pool of racial sorrow, the collective pain of

4

humanity. This is what makes it a great, enduring art form, because it transcends the specific circumstances of its creation and reaches out through time and space to touch the lives of people everywhere. We hunger for what is real, and the blues delivers. It eschews emotional posturing and vain technical flair and dives straight to the heart of the matter: the unshakable dilemma of being human. The original bluesmen and women lived and breathed and ate and slept the blues. It bled from their fingertips as they slid along the guitar strings; it poured out of them at the slightest opportunity for communal healing, taking whatever form was necessary.

In Shri, we play the blues for the same reasons: to release our burden of pain and anguish and connect with others through music. Deborah recalls how she first started singing the blues:

> The way that I started singing was to my children. Over ten years ago, I was in this really difficult, painful marriage and I had four kids to take care of, aged one, two, four and five. That was probably the hardest time of my life—I was emotionally very unstable. But every night when I put the kids to bed I had this ritual where I would lie down next to each child and I would ask them, "What song would you like me to sing you tonight?" I had a small repertoire of blues songs mostly, like *Summertime* and *You Got to Move.* Every night each child would get a couple of songs. Sometimes everyone would want the same one.
>
> That was where I really learned how to sing, singing to each child, because sometimes that was the only way I could express my concern and caring to these children, three of whom weren't my own. That was a place where we all could really connect. Maybe

all during the day things would be really emotionally chaotic, but when I would lie down with those children and sing it was just pure communication. So I really started singing as an act of love for my children, and to soften the rough edges of very difficult times.

I love this story because it explains what people feel from Deborah when she sings: that for her, making music is really an act of love.

Like many great singers, Deborah grew up using music as a spiritual anchor point to get her through the difficulties of her youth. She is most attracted to performers who are able to expose their most intimate feelings with power and simplicity, free of sentimentality— like Big Mama Thornton, Janis Joplin and Aretha Franklin. When she sings, people commonly feel as if she's singing right to them, telling her story as if it just happened on the way to the club. Maybe it's her years of experience as a nurse, tuning into people's needs and assuaging their fears. For her, singing the blues cultivates a compassion for humanity:

> Everybody's in the same amount of pain, even if they live in the suburbs and have a comfortable life. They just don't know they're in pain. It's like that old line that goes, "What you gonna do when your trouble gets like mine?" Your trouble already is like mine. We're all in the same boat. If you allow yourself to open up you're going to feel the misery that's been there forever. These blues songs are really honest, perfect descriptions of the human condition.

Historically, the exact genesis of the blues is forever lost to us:

true to its own spirit, the blues is like a motherless child. Existentially however, we know exactly where the blues comes from. We approach this music not simply as a twelve-bar song form with a certain rhythmic, harmonic and lyric structure that arose in the Mississippi Delta around 1900; it is the cry of the heart, naked and unadorned, seeking solace in its bereavement. It is a real wound and it seeks a real healing. Singing these lyric poems, drenched with bittersweet beauty and painful irony, is the heart's spontaneous movement toward easing its burden.

> I walked all the way from East St. Louis
> from East St. Louis here
> And I got nobody
> No one to feel my care.
> —Traditional[4]

And the message of the blues spread: the shouts and hollers of the cotton fields never stopped, but continued encircling the earth to hold us all in their embrace. It was a message we needed, because Western society was in a dead-end situation. Twentieth century America as well as many other technology-based cultures are characterized by a deep existential unease. Life has been getting faster and faster: Mom and Pop have moved off the farm to the big city, while the cosmopolitans have escaped to suburban wastelands; technology dominates more and more of our daily lives; total nuclear annihilation is still a threat; crime and pollution have reached levels beyond our control. Finally, the family, the most basic institution of our lives, is breaking down. Now, all we have left is the last stand of the individual against a host of problems that send most of us running to the nearest bottle of whatever it is that blots out our pain. No wonder that watching television has become an international pastime.

Many of the difficult problems in the black community that pervaded the early blues songs—the breakdown of the family, uprootedness, isolation, and the despair that comes with the loss of cultural values and rituals that bind people together—are now prevalent in contemporary life. Maybe that is one reason for the strange appeal of the blues of late. Why else would Robert Johnson's scratchy old recordings have sold over half a million copies this decade? The poetry of the blues is finally finding a crack in our facade of endless progress, as an unnamable anomie has crept into modern life.

> When the blues overtake me, gonna grab that train
>   and ride.
>
> When a woman get blue, she hang her head and cry.
> When a man get blue, he grab that train and ride.
>
> Yonder come that train, red-blue light behind.
> Red for trouble, blues for a worried mind.
>
> If you've ever been down, you know just how I feel.
> I feel like an engine ain't got no drivin' wheel.
>   —Traditional[5]

America was built on its railroad system, and scores of blues songs celebrate the freedom that riding the rails brought to the black culture (you can hear the boxcars rolling in the typical blues beat), just as, half a century later, scores of rock and roll songs would celebrate the freedom of racing down the highway in a sleek convertible. But, as Lee our lyricist says, "Freedom is just loneliness in drag."[6]

Young black men didn't wander about for their leisure—they were forced to because of the harsh realities of the land of their birth. And middle-class white America didn't start wandering about

8

the country for no reason either: they were missing something also. In this case the emptiness was in the spiritual domain, a loss of soul or heart that drained life of richness, depth and meaning. By the 1960s Americans were seriously on the move—it was a time when many of the youth turned to traditional blues music for inspiration because it embodied this restless spirit.

We are all adrift on the same ship of fools. We have all, black and white, lost touch with our ancestral roots, with the land, with our cultural heritage and ultimately with ourselves. But it is the African American who felt this sense of loss most deeply because he arrived here in shackles; he left his home against his will and remained here in bondage. Today, the heartbeat of Africa still pulsates in the rhythms of all great African American music—blues, jazz and gospel. It is this connection to their primal roots which pulls on our hearts and stirs our vitals, sparking feelings we didn't know we had.

The Blues Are Real

If this book's message could be summed up in one line, here it is: the blues are real. They are not a commodity, not some record company's idea of what the public will buy; they were here, in us, long before record companies existed, and they will be around long after. The blues arise out of a soul which has tasted the depth of what a human being can feel. When one is full of life and brimming over with feeling, pain and pleasure can reach such an unbearable intensity that they merge into a singular mood: ecstatic longing.

For Shri, the blues is a sacred prayer at a profane altar, a Dionysian rite, a lancing of a timeless wound, a celebration of pure fucking devoid of egoic display and sentimental gestures. The blues isn't the blues if it's not dangerous. Singing the blues, loving the blues, living the blues—it's like falling for the one you know will end up breaking your heart. But you just can't stop yourself.

John Lee Hooker, the King of the Boogie, knows how deep these blues get:

> It is the first music that was here . . . It is the one to tell the story of a human being or a man and a woman. Who started this? Eve and Adam in the Garden. When the blues was born it was born with Eve and Adam.[7]

With that kind of understanding, Hooker doesn't need scholars to enlighten him about the history of the blues. He *is* the blues. He and all the other great blues artists have lived the blues so profoundly that it simply oozes out of their pores. They couldn't stop themselves from singing the blues if they wanted to. As Johnny Shines says, "The blues are not wrote; the blues are lived."[8] And human beings have been living them since the beginning of time. All great music—in fact, all true art—arises from these blues, the heart's quaking contact with the awesome spectacle of life, the unstoppable cycle of creation and destruction which we ignore at our own peril.

The blues, as Willie Dixon often said, are simply the "facts of life," and the fact is that human life is filled with trials and troubles from the moment we are wrenched from our mother's womb, to our trembling hour of death. Our entire life is framed by these two points of impenetrable mystery, birth and death, and the stuff in the middle isn't much easier to get a grip on. To confront life head on (or to be confronted *by* life head on, which is usually how it feels) can leave us desperately trying to assign meaning and logic to events that are ultimately beyond our control. We pretend we have it all together, that we know where we are, where we're going, but the blues sweeps away our grandiose illusions to show us where we are really standing—we're on a lonely street corner at night, it's raining, and we're waiting for someone, anyone, to give us a ride.

We in Shri see a lot of worried people in our travels, especially when we play those bars on the other side of the tracks, so to speak, where the people have a "reason" to drink. These bars are full of crusty characters who convince me of the reality of suffering: imposing men with weapons bulging under black leather jackets, bone-thin women in revealing lace ready to throw their hearts at anyone who will comfort them for one lonely night, and alcohol-drenched old men staving off their encroaching death with the next swig of hard liquor. The edge of ever-impending violence and sexual desperation in these bars is usually enough to shock me out of my middle-class trance of comfort and control, as I realize that this dark underbelly of life I see all around me is also *in me*. Sometimes we have our hottest gigs in these places, because the people there are really yearning for something to lift them out of their dreary lives, and they are actually starving for an honest acknowledgment of their reality of suffering. When they receive that acknowledgment, something inside them relaxes, they lose their preoccupation with themselves and begin to look around, like it's suddenly safe to rejoin the world. But they can only receive that gift if those of us onstage are honest enough to embrace our own suffering, to admit how easy it would have been for one of us to be slouched over the bar in an alcoholic stupor, if the cards had been dealt differently.

In his book, *The Spirituals and the Blues*, Stephen Cone says that, ". . . the blues are that mood which owes its origins to powerlessness in the face of troubles."[9] What could be more troubling than the realization that everyone is born to die. We wonder: "Why was I born?" "Why do I have to die?" "Why do innocent people suffer?" "Why is true love so elusive?" It seems that helplessness is our constant companion from cradle to grave. These questions are at the core of the blues, and there isn't a human being on the face of the planet who can't relate to them.

B.B. King talked poignantly about how the blues is not just about his own pain, but about the pain of the world:

> We all have the blues. Red, white, black, brown, yellow—rich, poor—we all have these blues. You can be successful and still have the blues. I have been fortunate, and yet now I have more to sing about than ever . . . I think of my people, the ones I left behind in Mississippi, and all the people in all the Mississippis. We are a part of each other you know . . . When one person is hurt, it hurts me too. When I see their condition, I know what they feel, and I feel it, and it hurts.[10]

Maybe that's why B.B. is commonly called the "King of the Blues": not only for his seminal guitar style, or his rich, smooth vocal delivery, but for his heartfulness, his recognition of the basic dignity and interconnectedness of humanity. His commanding stage presence is fed by this well of compassion.

With the blues, instead of the person communicating the music, the music communicates the person; the audience is responding not only to the story that's being told and the notes that are being played, but to a flesh and blood human being. It is the sincerity, passion and love that this person has brought to his life and relationships that impact us through the music. And the blues is *the* style of American music that values those qualities above all else. African Americans tenaciously held onto these bedrock virtues, and their absolute refusal to let go of their human dignity in the face of abject cruelty and despair infuses their music with a healing balm. Richard Wright, in the foreword of Paul Oliver's *The Meaning of the Blues*, wrote:

> . . . the most astonishing aspect of the blues is
> that though replete with a sense of defeat and down-
> heartedness, they are not intrinsically pessimistic;
> their burden of woe and melancholy is dialectically
> redeemed through sheer force of sensuality into an
> almost exultant affirmation of life, of love, of sex, of
> movement, of hope.[11]

When our "spirits" are down, we still got "soul." Soul is not necessarily damaged by suffering, but actually can become stronger,
deeper and richer through hardship. It is as if the weight of our bur-
dens grounds us in reality, dragging us down into the bowels of the
earth where we are surprised to find a powerful healing force.

Deborah talked about one night at a club when she felt this ability of the blues to translate our suffering into an affirmation of life.
As she described it:

> I was having a relatively normal week, when sud-
> denly several crises at once all seemed to converge on
> me. We had a gig that evening, and I had no idea how
> I was going to make it through the night because I
> was emotionally spent. Just to stand onstage and open
> my mouth was a huge endeavor. Then we got to the
> Big Mama Thornton song, *Ball and Chain,* and some-
> thing shifted. It was just like the song says, one
> moment I was moving along, and then here comes all
> sorts of trouble, like a ball and chain. At that
> moment I felt like nothing was ever more true than
> that song, and I was singing it like never before . . .

I became one with it. Then I looked around at all the people in the audience and I realized they were in the same exact place as me—at any moment, life could throw them into breakdown and turmoil. Right then, in the midst of my own suffering, and being able to see the same suffering in the faces of the people in the audience, seeing how we were all working this thing out together . . . well, that was when I found out what the blues was all about.

This is the kind of healing ceremony one might not expect to take place in a dark, smoky bar; but in one way, bars really are a perfect place to confront the murky aspects of our humanity, because there we can let it all hang out in plain view. This is why Wright refers to the blues as the "spirituals of the city pavements,"[12] for it shares with its cousin, the great black spirituals, the ability to transform the fire of suffering into the heat of love. Yet it achieves this not through some supernatural transcendence of this world, but through fully accepting it, even diving into it. The blues are almost unique in being a thoroughly secular music that is nevertheless infused with an unmistakable spiritual feeling. They have been called "secular spirituals,"[13] because they achieve a "transformation of . . . life through the sheer power of song."[14]

The Blues as World Music

The irresistible appeal of the blues is its ability to embrace *all* of life. In this, it shares a common thread with another great folk tradition, Spanish flamenco music, the *cante jondo* (literally, "deep song") of the Gypsies of Andalusia. The Gypsies are another people who have endured untold persecution, have held onto their dignity and love of

life, and have expressed this through incredibly passionate music that
has swept across their entire nation, and now the world. The poet
Frederico Garcia Lorca beautifully described the Gypsy's haunting
song of the tragic sense of life, when he wrote:

> See for yourselves the transcendent quality of
> cante jondo . . . It is deep . . . deeper than the present
> heart that composes it or sings it, because it is almost
> infinite. It comes from distant races, crossing the
> cemetery of the years and the leaves of shriveling
> winds. Born of the first cry . . .[15]

"Born of the first cry . . ." That in itself suffices for a definition
of the blues. Undoubtedly, if we didn't have a music like the blues or
cante jondo, we would have to invent one. The heart's cry will not be
silenced, extinguished, nor rationalized out of existence. It is what
most makes us human, and it is what allows all the disparate peoples
of the planet to ultimately understand each other. John Lee Hooker
echoes Lorca's sentiment about the power of music to transcend the
personal: "It's somewhere down the line that you have been hurt
some place . . . It's not only what happened to you—it's what happened to your foreparents and other people."[16]

I have felt this power of music to transcend cultural, racial and
religious boundaries, which makes it especially difficult to listen to
those who claim that whites can never hope to truly play or even
appreciate the blues, that different races can never really communicate or understand each other. Those who make this statement ignore
the sincere homage, praise and even devotion that many white musicians have shown for this music. Johnny Shines, Robert Johnson's
right hand man for several years, put it this way:

You see, blues don't have no race. Blues don't have
no level. The blues is just like death. Everybody is
going to have the blues. If they haven't already had
'em, they're gonna have 'em . . .You see whatsoever
touches the heart is where the blues comes from.[17]

John Lee Hooker agrees, when he says that "every person or race
has had these heartaches . . ."[18] As the famous line in the song *Five
Long Years* goes: "If you've ever been mistreated/you know just what
I'm talkin' about."[19] It takes someone who has been down to recognize that our hearts are all made of the same stuff.

A similar controversy has cropped up in Spain as well, where it is
said that only Gypsies can authentically perform the "deep song."
The celebrated flamenco master Pepe El de la Matrona echoes our
sentiment about the blues, saying, ". . . it is not important to know
if you are a payo or a gitano but to know how to sing and nothing
else."[20]

Ironically, music is one arena where not only blacks and whites,
but peoples all over the world have transcended tremendous differ-
ences. While armies are ripping each other to shreds, pickers and fid-
dlers are sneaking across enemy lines eagerly trading licks. The language of music bridges gaps where the languages of politics, psychology, philosophy and religion fail. This is simply because music
allows us to communicate on an essential level, a level of feeling,
which bypasses the level of mind where our fixed ideas, opinions and
expectations inevitably clash. The heart of the blues is so big, everyone can find a home in it; and the language is so straightforward that
anyone can relate to it. Charles Simic said that the blues:

> . . . prove the complete silliness of any theory of
> cultural separatism which decries the possibility of

aesthetic experience outside one's race, ethnicity, religion, or even gender. Like all genuine art, the blues belongs to a specific time, place, and people which it then, paradoxically, transcends.[21]

That explains how this music from the deep South could pop up, of all places, in England. In the early 1960s, young men from shabby, industrial cities started a small but powerful blues movement which, in a matter of years, sparked the British invasion, the ascendancy of rock and roll, and a renewal of interest in the blues in the U.S. as well. This music has definitely shown an ability to rise beyond the cultural constraints of it past. The blues has always been about transcendence.

Erica Jong, in her book on Henry Miller, says that to ". . . define the self in a world that is hostile to the very notion of your selfhood is still every woman writer's challenge."[22] This aptly describes the challenge of the original blues artists as well—the color of their skin was enough to erase, in the eyes of society, their identity as human beings. But the dehumanizing effects of a culture that values money and power over soul and compassion are not felt by one race alone. Everyone in this country is at the effect of the same spiritual emptiness that reduces living, breathing, hurting, laughing human beings to commodities. Yes, there are many whose born advantages have enabled them to build up enough material and psychological comfort to shield them from the ordinary troubles of life that affect us all. But the moment tragedy strikes them, it is as if they are stripped of everything they had spent their whole lives attaining, and are suddenly reduced to vulnerable, frightened and lonely men or women.

The blues arose from the pain of a people who had been stripped down to the core of their being, and they speak to that same place inside all of us, the place underneath all the ways we defend ourselves and make ourselves comfortable. The original blues singers certainly had no way, as many of us today do, of denying the unending spiritual ache that gnawed away at their tattered existence. Their music is a lament of an utterly lost and bereft people, a miracle of paralyzing despair transformed into an affirmation of the human spirit, a spirit that seemed to actually become stronger as the blues of life were transformed through the blues of song. There is an alchemical power that is built into blues music, and all it needs is a singer/musician with a depth of being to unleash it, and an audience with a depth of being to receive it. When we listen to the blues, that one inside us who is listening—the naked, vulnerable person—is our real self, the one we've been trying so hard to hide, and the same one we'd give anything to reveal.

The Cauldron of Slavery

Although it is true that everyone suffers, it must be acknowledged that the Delta Blues were forged out of suffering and cruelty the likes of which most of us will never know nor cannot even imagine. The Mississippi Delta, the area that birthed the vast majority of seminal blues figures in the early 1900s, was said to be "one of the most vicious areas of human intolerance and brutality on the face of the earth . . ."[23] It was an isolated area, and the white landowners squeezed every nickel they could out of the poor blacks who were stuck there. The music we know as the blues actually arose a generation or two after the fall of the Confederacy in 1865, when the blacks' newfound freedom meant little more than the total breakdown of whatever semblance of community life they had on the plantation. As far as real economic, educational or political opportunities, they had achieved virtually nothing, and in fact were more economically and socially insecure than ever. The basic foundation of community life, values and ritual—the family—broke down, as men, women and children were forced to wander the desolate flat plains of the Delta, looking for any work they could get. It was not uncommon for boys to leave home at the tender age of nine, ten or twelve, wandering off into a dangerous world with the vague hope of a better life.

The post-Civil-War South was an environment that was physically threatening and spiritually devastating for blacks, and those whose job it was to uphold the law were definitely not on their side. In the deep South, merely looking at a white woman could get a black man sentenced for rape (a life sentence), and smiling at someone the wrong way was grounds for a civil disobedience rap. Itinerant workers who were unlucky enough to get caught wandering in an area where the county needed some work done, could be plucked off the road and forced into a work camp. Reason: vagrancy. (So much for new found freedom.) These men could be beaten or killed if they didn't work hard enough in these thinly veiled prisons, and were routinely cheated out of their meager pay. There was absolutely no one to turn to for justice.

Levee camps existed all along the Mississippi River from Memphis, Tennessee to Vicksburg, Mississippi, about a 200-mile stretch. This area, commonly called the Delta, is technically not a river delta but a flat plain that was made fit for farming by the damming of the great river with huge earthen walls (called levees), an awesome achievement of mostly African Americans, who, through inhumanly difficult work, converted an uninhabitable swamp into some of the richest farmland in the country. The levee is longer and wider than the Great Wall of China, the largest structure ever built by man. Yet, all that many of the blacks got for their achievement was slavery, imprisonment or death.

A common saying among the blacks in those days was, "Kill a

mule, buy another one. Kill a nigger, buy another one." In fact, mules, at four hundred dollars a beast, were actually more highly valued by the white landowners. And if one black worker killed another in one of the many fights that ensued in this tense and bitter atmosphere—well, that was OK with the boss, provided the corpse in question hadn't been a good worker. Guns or knives could break out at any time. One story goes that a gambler was killed during a fight over a hot game, and as he lay there, still warm, a shorter (and perhaps younger) patron stepped up on the body to follow the action at the table. Bodies were generally just thrown out back.

The levee camps had juke joints for Saturday night revelry, replete with music, moonshine, gambling and prostitution. This was the environment many blues singers experienced in their youth, and music to them was more than a pastime—it was a matter of their survival: both spiritually, to remind themselves that they were digni- fied human beings who had heart, and physically, to provide a means of making a living that could carry them out of this unholy land. These were maybe the first venues that blues performers had, as the genre was just coming out of the fields where it had existed for gen- erations as worksongs or "hollers."

Singing while working is still common today in most areas of Africa where the weave of tribal life has not been undone through industrialization. In America too, sharecroppers would sing lone- some tunes as they plowed their fields*, songs about their troubles: the intense heat of the Mississippi sun beating down; the money they owed to the white landowners, which kept them tied to a place that was no home; the many children they had to feed. The blacks in America continued the tradition of making song a part of everyday life, but here the music was suffused with pain and anguish, because

*Fields recordings of these African and African American field songs reveal eerily similar melodies.

that *was* daily life. To open one's mouth in the middle of a field and just sing out one's pitiful song to the furrowed earth and the wind and the wide sky was all that they had "in place of freedom."[24] Alan Lomax said that, "African American singers and dancers made an aesthetic conquest of their environment in the New World."[25] I would add that aesthetics for African Americans are inseparable from a sense of spirituality and communal ritual, so that their conquest was more informed by an abiding connection to a deep spiritual spring than mere aesthetic principles.

Sunnyland Slim, the legendary piano player, when asked where the blues began, replied firmly that the blues ". . .started from slavery."[26] The identification of the origin of the blues with slavery and racism was obvious to the black men and women who sang them. Lonesome Jimmy said that ". . . this people they had so much torment—lynched, burned, tarred and feathered . . . they have sung sadder blues than we could ever imagine."[27] Johnny Shines gave us probably the best description we could have, so I will quote him at length.

> When you hear people singing hymns in church—these long, drawn out songs—that's the blues. Yeah. Church music and the blues is all one and the same. They come out of the same soul, same heart, same body. The division come back in slavery times when slaves were singing these mournful, lonesome songs. The slaves didn't know anything about "blues" or "church songs" at that time.
>
> We were brought over here as slaves. We didn't bring . . . no sheet music—nothing but what we remembered in our minds. What happened to the older ones that were brought over here? They were soon dead, because what man from Africa had

learned how to get out and work twelve and fourteen and fifteen hours a day carrying logs, cleaning up ground, and digging ditches . . . It took a younger man who had to be hardened as he come along. And these were the men who were singing the blues, even though they didn't call it that.

They learned English. They sang songs about . . . the way they was living . . . these people didn't even have no clothes to change into! Lice ate them up, you understand? And they was full of disease. And . . . they didn't call in no doctors . . .

Then these people singing these songs begun to be noticed. The white people started asking, "What's wrong with these people? Why is they singing?" They didn't know these people really was praying, that every time they opened their mouth was a prayer coming out . . . So how could it be called "blues" or how could it be called "church songs?" They asked, "What's wrong with these people? They sound like they have tears in their voices."

So the masters held a meeting about it—said, "We got to . . . [t]ell these people, 'Don't sing those songs. Don't sing about your state of being. Sing about John the Baptist over the sea. Sing about the holy city—Jerusalem. You'll be so happy when you get over the river Jordan.'" The white people taught them these kind of songs. They taught them the Bible. They stopped them from singing about being beat and full of lice, and sickness, and death, and sold.

Just think of a little child standing at his mother's

knee, crying, "Mama, take me up." And she can't even look down at him. She got to look the people in the eye who's gonna sell her and buy her. "Mama, please, I want some titty, Mama." She can't even reach down and pick him up and nurse him. Now, those people had the blues!

When they told them they shouldn't sing these songs, they told them they was reels. "Don't sing those reels or you'll die and go to hell and burn forever and ever." And then they went on later to relate those reels to syphilis, sex, murder, getting drunk—you understand what they mean? And naturally the people believed them. Who else was there to believe in?

If you killed another black man, they'd just say, "We got to split his land up between you and so-and-so . . . cause he's dead now."

"Yassuh, I'll take it. I'll work it."

Sing about that. That's the real blues.[28]

Yet, even in the face of horrifying circumstances like these, many still affirm that "the actual physical brutalities of slavery were minor in comparison to the loss of community."[29] This is because community provides a kind of nurturance and sanctuary where soul can flourish and actually remain strong in the face of otherwise unbearable torment. There are many stories from World War II concentration camps, for instance, that show that community, service, selfless sharing and love can save lives.

But when slavery ended, blacks were confronted with the same world of racial intolerance and poverty *without* the community that the plantation provided. Thrust from the self-contained world of the plantation, blacks found themselves in an extremely different environment where the "we" subsided into the background, and the "I" gained glorious prominence. This must have been shocking to the core for a people who had known only a self identified with community for untold generations. I would contend that it was this sudden immersion into the Western worship of individuality that produced what we now call "the Blues." Cast out of his communal world, the "free" black man wanders bewildered, bereft, alone. The psychological landscape suddenly changes from a living green ecosystem to a desolate plain, dotted with isolated trees. The "I" is too great a burden without the support and bonding of the community. The blues are born.

Here we enter the strata of human experience that engenders all great artistic endeavors, and all authentic religious ritual as well—our struggle to come to terms with our suffering and accept our fate on earth, while at the same time longing for an experience of healing and wholeness. If it were not for suffering, there would be no motivation to examine our lives, question its meaning, and strive for a better world. All the great spiritual traditions acknowledge the value and necessity of suffering. "All life is suffering" is the first law of Buddhism, the first lesson one encounters on the spiritual path. To experience the heights of joy and ecstasy, one must also be open to the depths of pain. Heartbreak becomes a doorway to God.

Alan Lomax, the great ethnomusicologist and champion of the Delta blues, recently remarked that:

> . . . great art has always come when people are
> held under a hell of pressure and have to deal with
> great difficulties and transform whatever they got,
> their toothpick or their little flute or whatever they
> have in a statement of defiance against death and

destruction and demoralization and hate.[30]

The art of people in these situations is not a political statement butting against hostile forces; rather, it is a courageous declaration of their innate dignity as human beings. Music for African Americans was a way of staying connected to soul, spirit and God.

A Collision of Cultures

At the turn of the twentieth century, America was well on its way to its great technological conquest of the world. In the span of a decade we saw the birth of the automobile, the airplane and the moving picture. And while the Western world stood marveling at these paradigm-shattering changes, another development was taking place in an isolated, backwater section of the South known as the Mississippi Delta that would become just as powerful a force. It rose up out of the soul of a people to answer a need. As jazz musician Noble Sissie says, the music " . . . did not just happen . . . There is a history to the birth of our music. There is almost every element of life in it—religion, romance, tragedy, faith, hope and primitive abandon—brought together and paid for at a tremendous price."[31]

To my knowledge, Amiri Baraka, in his seminal work *Blues People*, grasped better than anyone this monumental moment when these two worldviews met. African slavery had existed for centuries, but slaves in Africa were still considered human beings by their masters, a situation more similar to the system of indentured servants in Europe. But when African men, women and children crossed the Atlantic Ocean, they were reduced from living, breathing, feeling, thinking human beings to mere commodities—in the eyes of many of their "masters," something like a talking ox. This was because the Western worldview was so different from the African, and the

Westerners were totally convinced that their view was the right one. So, the Africans were faced with a situation that forced them to squeeze their sensitive, multidimensional, deeply feeling selves into a cultural straightjacket. "To be brought to a country, a culture, a society, that was, and is . . . the complete antithesis of one's own version of man's life on earth—that is the *cruelest* aspect of this particular slavery."[32]

The Puritans, the first European settlers upon American soil, set the tone for everything that followed. The poet William Carlos Williams described the Puritans as a strange and inhuman lot, although powerful. They represented the final death blow of Western philosophy upon the sacredness of bodily ecstasy, for, in their view, music, dance, sex and play were basically not included as essential or even *good* aspects of human life. An African person at that time would probably wonder, "Why live at all?" The Puritans believed in predestination: they held that there were only a certain number of "elect" who had already been chosen, and that there was nothing they could do about it. The only thing left to do in life was to work and make money, because, in some twisted, bizarre way, economic prosperity was regarded as proof that one was "saved" and going to heaven. Puritanism ranks among the most depressing philosophies that this planet has produced, and it was the first one to be widely practiced in America. Think about that.

Baraka goes even further to say that, ". . . colonial America was the country of the new post-Renaissance man, the largest single repository for humanism in the New World."[33] They practiced ". . . the exaltation of secular man." We had reduced the goals of life to such a pedestrian level that we became a nation of bookkeepers, magistrates and traffic cops. Humanism trumpeted that man was the sole measure of all things great and small, the earth was the center of the universe, and the entire universe (galaxies and all) was created just for him, so God could follow his every movement throughout his important life and judge whether he should be damned to eternal torment or blessed with eternal bliss. And what is ironic is that these "humanists" were the same people who denigrated the highly complex and sensitive religious beliefs of the Africans as utterly ignorant, debased and savage.

It is significant that Westerners tended to view the music of the Africans in much the same light, for music has an inherent power to embody and communicate the essential worldview of the performers. H.E. Krehbiel was bewildered that ". . . savages who have never developed a musical or other art [!!!] should be supposed to have more refined aesthetic sensibilities than the peoples who have cultivated music for centuries. . . "[34] And Harold Courlander, in his book *Haiti Singing*, quotes an observer of Haitian ritual: "All the more undisguised is the crude sensuality among the lower classes . . . Here every motion is obscene . . . [the dances] are more like orgies, in which the African savagery, which has outlived centuries, has unbridled expression."[35] It seems clear that the pure terror of "unbridled" ecstatic bodily expression is what really underlies the insipid arrogance of the quote by Krehbiel. The only way a person (and there were many) could listen to African or African American music and proclaim that these were "savages who have never developed a musical . . . art," is if he or she was completely divorced from their own bodily life—joy, pain, terror and longing—and ultimately from their own humanity.

Ironically, as the Puritans and their "spiritual" kin were decrying the lack of religion in the poor, ignorant savages, it was they and not the slaves who were suffering from a spiritual deficiency, for to be cut off from one's bodily life is to experience a kind of soul loss. The effect is emotionally and spiritually devastating, for those who cannot feel their own pain are completely immune to feelings of true compassion as well, and they will take out their sense of shame and self-loathing on others through a harsh disciplinary attitude and the inculcation of life-choking rules of conduct.

Alan Lomax spoke of the southern whites and ". . . the melancholy desperation with which their sin-haunted religion and their inflexible racism filled the hearts of their black neighbors."[36] It is quite possible that the suffering of the African American slaves was rooted in this sick Western shame and hatred of the physical body. Those who naturally inhabit their bodies with joy and unselfconsciousness—among whom are children, women, and "savages"—are generally the first targets for this life-negative "education." Those who have no joy hate more than anything to see others who do, and they will do anything they can to wipe that joy out. Still today, ultra-conservatives fight to ban certain types of music; they recognize instinctively that music is dangerous because it is the most potent force for communicating this *joie de vivre.* The history of black music (and black-inspired music, like rock and roll) is a chronicle of praise and grateful embrace on one side of the aisle, and frowns of disapproval, shock and cries of outrage on the other. For some, it is too threatening to have their comfortable fortress of defense against life crumble, while others are busy dancing in the streets and thanking God for a milieu in which to express their long-withheld feelings. The blues seeks simply to expose and clarify all the facets of a human being, especially the primal energies of the body; those who feel threatened by it are convinced that the fate of their soul depends on fighting back these untamed beasts roaming within them. America has long been a battle ground for these two forces (and still is!). For a long time we have been the land both of the free-spirited as well as those who feel that, as Americans, we have a moral high-ground to uphold.

The Voice of the Ancestors

The original blues artists' parents and grandparents had been slaves, and their ancestors only a few generations back came from Africa. The oral tradition was crucial for the survival of their culture and therefore their souls, and this tradition was most often expressed in song. The white masters intuitively understood that the music of the Africans carried a strange power that they didn't understand, and they were determined to get rid of it: they banned drumming. America was the only New World destination of the slaves where drumming was forbidden, and it also became the only place where African religion all but died out, because drumming was essential to ritual. Julio Finn, in *The Bluesman*, made the crucial point that the spirituality of the African people had to find a place to go, and one of the places it found a home was in their music.

For African Americans, music was a way of reconstituting their communal ritual life in a land that prohibited any overt expression of their strong spiritual beliefs. We shall see in the following pages that although their music may have lost much of the form and content of this ritual life, it has retained the distinct mood and flavor of it. Religion and music are both essential to human life, focal points in practically every culture we know of. If the African Americans were deprived of their religion, it only made their music stronger, that much more evocative of primordial spirituality. The gods of Africa took up residence in the blues, because music has always been the way for the Africans to call down their gods. Now they needed their help more than ever.

C h a p t e r   2

African Roots

By far the most important single factor in African music is
the full recognition and practical . . . use of the
metaphysical powers of Sound.

—Fela Sowande[1]

Shri Gets the Spirit

In the summer of 1996, our band Shri played at the Nice Jazz
Festival in the south of France. Before our show we walked the territory checking out some other acts for inspiration. One group from
Mississippi captured our attention. The Canton Spirituals were eight
men dressed in their Sunday best, their ages spanning three generations. The warmth they all exuded toward one another had the feel of
an extended family.

Their set started off slow and sweet as their rich, deep voices
gently stirred the crowd. As they sang, I could see them going deep
within themselves, mining for the ore of true feeling, notes of liquid
gold transforming the muddy tent into a regal house of worship.
These men were masters at working a crowd, slowly building the
energy so that no one knew what hit them. Then they gradually shifted from the slow, sweet numbers to more blues- and funk-driven

grooves. Now they were strutting across the stage showing their stuff; what looked like an angelic choir was really a bunch of guys who wanted to get down and get funky. And there was no problem bridging the gap; they were singing about their relationship to God, yet they had no shame, no desire to hide their sexuality.

Another evening as we wandered about we heard jubilant uplifting voices coming from another stage, *Les Arenes*, an ancient Gallo-Roman coliseum fitted with a modern P.A. system. As we approached I could see and feel the heat coming off the place. Everyone in the audience of two thousand was clapping with enthusiasm, as deep feminine voices filled the air, weaving a bright tapestry of joy, hope and longing. I wondered at the irony of this kind of jubilation taking place within these crumbling, ivy-choked walls, where perhaps almost two thousand years ago Christians were fed to hungry lions. Now the tables were turned! Six black women, powerful and commanding, had the audience totally under their spell. The ladies were all dressed in proper black skirts and jackets with silver trim and blue velvet high-heeled shoes sprinkled with rhinestones. The raw energy that radiated from them was shocking, and the French audience was responding in kind by shouting, stomping, and letting *Hallelujahs* ring out into the night sky. Participating with the New Orleans Spiritualettes (one cannot simply watch them), we were swept up into a tribal ambiance.

"Praise Him!" the women sang call-and-response style, while others added in moans and cries as the spirit moved them. This was pure worship, completely unadorned with sentimentality or calculated musical showmanship. Most of these women were not young, yet they were giving everything they had; I could see the sweat pouring off them, and the fatigue on their faces when they stopped to take a breath. Some of them had kicked off their shoes, and their proud strong feet seemed to rise up out of the earth like tree trunks. They ran around stage inciting each other and the musicians to greater and greater degrees of self-abandon. A couple of them, who seemed to be the leaders of the pack, stepped offstage into the rocking and swaying crowd. They were great big short women who constantly went in and out of trancelike states, not holding back one ounce of their energy and love. They danced with people in the audience, making the spirit available to anyone who would put aside self-consciousness and approach them. The crowd was so primed and grateful for this opportunity to let go, to simply celebrate and praise without reservation, and to leave their lives of worry and complaint behind.

One of the sisters raised her arms to heaven, her hands vibrating madly, her head rolled back and eyelids closed; she swayed and swooned, surrendered to some higher force. Suddenly her body became limp and the other sister had to hold her up. The entranced woman was totally gone, possessed by a force beyond all understanding or control. In that instant I saw the heart of their show, the source of their communication. Here was the inspiration that those three thousand people were looking for in their lives. The show ended with the ladies inviting up several people onstage to dance, as they closed with the old standard *When the Saints Go Marchin' In*.

We all came away from that show stunned—cold and pale theories about music blown away by the depth of their communication and the force of their conviction. The mood that they left us with was nothing short of love.

Unfortunately, in our culture love is a word that has been battered and abused, sucked dry of meaning, candy-coated and generally misunderstood; yet, it is the only way to describe what these women were doing. The awesome force of the love that they were unleashing was undeniable. But rather than bask in its gentle glow, I was faced with my own habitual and persistent suffering, and the feelings of hopelessness that choked my heart. In short, being so totally immersed in an atmosphere of love showed me how I do not love. It became obvious that I spend most of my energy avoiding love, stubbornly refusing to serve others or to surrender to life's twists and turns gracefully. This big "NO" to life in myself was staring me in the face. More than providing me with a momentary feeling of emotional bliss, the New Orleans Spiritualettes gave me a greater gift: their music revealed my inner self with clarity and showed me where I have to work if I want to build more relationship in my life and my music.

After the show I told one of the lead women how much I appreciated what she had done for all of us. She thanked me, and then took my arm and said, "Pray for me." Then, she hobbled away into the night, exhausted, holding her rhinestone shoes and microphone, leaving me stunned once again. The depth of her humility struck a note of sorrow within me. I saw that this music was not coming from her desire to enlighten others, but out of her own need for God. This was her way of receiving help, her path to the heart of the Divine.

That festival was a revelation for me, as I realized the profound gift African American music has been for all of us. Again and again I was brought to tears by the sincerity of their heartfulness; I felt my spine tingle from the sheer force of their conviction; I broke out in ear-to-ear grins watching their playfulness; and I wondered in awe when a guitarist or singer would reach that point when "they" disappeared and what was left was pure spontaneous creative expression. This was initiation into the Mysteries, or at least as close as I had ever gotten. This was my church, my worship, not of some unknown, intangible, distant God; this was worship of the human being as the Divine. It wasn't elevating humanity to some transcendent level—this was it. This ordinary, fallible human being was made in God's image. That's what makes blues and gospel music so potent—its pain and its praise hits us where we live.

African Religion and African Music

Much has been made of the survival of traditional African musical styles in modern African American music. There are numerous examples: the polyrhythms of jazz, i.e., the existence of two distinct rhythmic elements at the same time; the call-and-response singing of the church; use of notes not represented by the Western scale system; and nearly identical dance forms. But none of these elements alone or taken as a whole can explain the profound and widespread effects that African American music has had on our culture. It was not simply a unique musical sensibility, but a completely different perspective on life that seduced and entranced the Western world.

Africans have highly complex and sensitive religious systems that encompass all areas of life, yet many books on world religions don't include a chapter on any African religions, and those few that do lump the beliefs of the entire continent together into one vague mass. There is a prejudice against religious traditions like those in Africa that are shaman-oriented, meaning that: 1) they value communal participation over complete dependence on priests; 2) they value the oral tradition over the written; 3) they value happiness in this world over perfection in the next; 4) they recognize a whole pantheon of gods and deities besides the one creator God; and 5) they encourage wild trance states and spirit possession rather than meditative equilibrium and control of the passions. All these values relegate the African's spirituality to the status of an uncivilized orgiastic cult in the eyes of many scholars in the West. This reactionary stance toward African religion underlies the negative response with which African-influenced music has sometimes been greeted.

In most African religions there is no artificial split between the world of spirit and the life of the body; the Divine is worshipped in and as the human body, the earth, and all of creation. It is primarily this perspective, seeping through the music with invisible force,

34

which is responsible for the awesome impact African American music has had on this century. The African worldview held that music, dance, sexuality and spirituality were all inextricably connected. Many tribes do not even have a separate word for music, because it is so much a part of everyday life. The blues has its roots in this world, where music helps to convey a profound sense of connection to the earth, the cycles of life, the tribe and oneself.

Many elements of African religious thought can be traced to African American music today. Michael Ventura points out that we can ". . . measure the strength of the metaphysics of Africa—we can gauge the depth of its relevance to the human condition every-where—by the bare fact that it survived through this centuries long ordeal."[2] Probably the greatest retention of African metaphysics within the blues is that salvation is not an other-worldly affair, but rather a here-and-now form of renewal and redemption. This was precisely the answer of the blues, where healing was often to be found in the domain of love and sex. Another African belief that crops up in the blues is the non-perfectability of human beings. This imparts an undeniably fatalistic flavor to the music, but it also leaves it refreshingly free of righteousness and shame.

Ironically, as the slaves in America were still singing traditional African songs that they had managed to pass down in their new "home," as well as newly-wrought spirituals encoded with messages about returning home to Africa, their African cousins were likewise singing songs about the loss that they felt. The following song is from a *griot*, a wandering bard of Northwest Africa, commonly referred to as the prototype of the African American bluesman.

> . . . When the Europeans came,
> when they brought their ship from Portugal,
> the ship used to start its journey from Banjul,

then it went to Sanumunko Jammeh, and Mansa
    Demba Sanko,
and Samkala Marong, and Wali Mandeba, and Jata
    Sela.
Anyone who had slaves they collected them all
    together
and took them to the places called Aladbara Jufure
to sell them to the Portuguese.
Then the Portuguese put them in their ship
and left there and went to Jang Jang Bure.
When they arrived there they went
right to the slave house to collect slaves there
and take them to the Hollanders.
Then the Hollanders collected them and sent them
    to America.
It is because of this
that slaves are plenty in America.

They call them American Negroes.
                                —From *The Song of Kanuteh*[3]

As the sole repository of tribal history, *griots* performed a unique and highly-valued function for their community. The bluesmen and women also performed a similar historical function, documenting through song events like the great flood at Natchez, Mississippi in 1929, the sinking of the Titanic, World Wars I and II, and the assassination of President Kennedy. In the case of the *griots*, their historical acumen also dovetailed into another more important function, that of communicating with the local tribal gods, who were often embodied in the spirits of the ancestors.

In the cosmology of many African religions, God the Absolute is seen as existing apart from his creation and unconcerned with the petty affairs of human beings; therefore, Africans appeal to lesser deities to provide guidance, power and blessings from the higher worlds. Africans believe that these deities are more interested in the daily affairs of earth, and they call upon them in times of sickness, family disputes or other crises, as well as in transitions such as birth, death and marriage. (For greater concerns like war or famine that involve the destiny of the entire tribe, they direct their supplications to the Creator.) Some ancestors who have achieved glory and fame on earth through heroic deeds have "graduated" to the status of minor deities in the afterlife. A strong relationship with these ancestors is seen as crucial for the health and functioning of the tribe. Here enters the *griot:* with an encyclopedic knowledge of everyone's family tree, he effectively possesses a skeleton key to the spiritual realms. He is entertainer, historian and priest rolled into one: in other religions he would be called a shaman.

According to tradition, the first *griot,* Sourakata, was the personal praise-singer of the Prophet Mohammed. He would wander about with Mohammed and his disciples, and when they entered a new town or village, he would announce the arrival of the Prophet with sacred songs. Mohammed received many gifts from the villagers, and he would lavish an inordinate amount of these upon Sourakata. When the other disciples got jealous of this unfair treatment, Mohammed ordered Sourakata to remain silent. When the Prophet and his entourage arrived at the next town there was no throng of excited and curious villagers bearing gifts; Sourakata had not proclaimed his coming and therefore no one in that town knew who they were. Thereafter, the disciples had to acknowledge Sourakata's important function.

Yet despite the *griots'* crucial social and religious function, they remain one of the lowest castes in West Africa, an area that has been extensively Islamicized. Frequently, *griots* have no permanent home and wander about to make a living. Islam recognizes only one God, and conversing with spirits is understandably looked at askance, a relic of a more primitive era. However, the spirit of the old religions still informs the lives of most Africans: for example, even though Muslims say drumming brings evil, they still use drums to ". . . drive away evil spirits, bring rain, and [accompany] circumcision rites."[4]

The *griot* is a walking link with these older ways; to this day, the presence of the *griot* is required at most weddings, births and deaths: all points of intersection with the spirit. The mixture of old and new religions explains how Africans can simultaneously honor and scorn the *griot*. In this way he is a close cousin with the American bluesman who, while generally relegated to the bottom of the societal heap, was nevertheless welcomed with enthusiasm by the common folk wherever his travels led him.

> Indeed, the griots, such as the virtuosic bards of Senegal . . . still play a leading role in the life of many West African communities . . . they are social satirists, whose verses once on a time dethroned chieftains. The bluesman of the delta continued this satiric tradition, depicting, as far as he dared, the ills and ironies of life in his caste-ridden society. Musicologists generally agree that America's black bluesmen have, in essence, reconstituted the high art of the African griot.[5]

Griots are not only praise singers; they know all the gossip, and this makes people a little leery of them.

A Day in the Life

Rows of neatly-woven thatched huts sit peacefully in the relentless Senegal sun. Children are running about, clapping and singing, playing musical games. Women sit in groups weaving, cooking and chatting while the old ones sit in the shade, quietly watching, occasionally telling stories or singing songs. Most of the men are off tending the fields, their work songs floating into the village on a dry wind. In the distance, a group of hens scatters off clucking and fussing as a group of strangers approach. The leader is a tall man with jet-black skin, his dark purple robe almost trailing the dusty ground. Slung over his left shoulder is a dried up gourd with a long neck attached, along which float five metal strings. It is called a *halam*, said to be an instrument of the angels, whose notes sound like "wind through the trees in heaven."[6] His countenance is regal, yet his caravan is quite modest: one small rickety wagon carries his extended family and all their possessions. A few scrawny goats trail behind.

The group stops short of the gathering throng of curious villagers, while the man walks confidently through the crowd, straight up to the village elders. His eyes are piercing, yet they don't rest anywhere for long; instead they seem to sink down into some great spaciousness within him. He speaks a few short, quiet words. The elders immediately respond: "Yes, a little one has died. Some evil illness brought by the Portuguese. You may perform the ceremonies." Arrangements for payment (a few of the chickens which previously scattered before him) and a place to stay are quickly settled.

The family of the dead child and the elders are relieved at his arrival; they seemed to almost expect him, even though no message was sent. Others in the village are mistrustful and keep their distance. Some even spit in his path.[7] His kind are not fit to be buried in the sacred ground; when a *griot* dies, his body is stuffed into the hollow trunk of a baobab tree, where it is soon devoured by hungry jackals.

(Bluesmen often expressed their fear about proper burial; e.g., Blind Lemon Jefferson's *Please See That My Grave is Kept Clean*.) *Griots* are said to practice sorcery and converse with evil spirits, and people fear the power of those who are able to invoke *jinn* and obtain their blessings (or curses). Yet, at times like these, they are more than ready to acknowledge and use his expertise.

As his family settles into their accommodations, the *griot* finds a suitable spot and begins to tune his *halam*, the sacred instrument used to accompany all his songs. His son, apprenticing in this tradition since the age of eight, sits beside him with his own smaller *halam*, receiving instruction on what to play. The songs will start at sunset and continue until sunset the following day. The *griot* will sing about the dead boy's ancestors and praise their exploits, digging deep into time past. He will sing about the Prophet Mohammed and his teachings, about life and death, good and evil. Finally he will document the coming of the white man and their dark gift which claimed this young boy's life. The *griot's* epic song will weave the dead child's life into a greater whole and give it meaning for the whole tribe, and this story will be passed on to future generations of *griots*.

After an entire day of song and stories, the mourning is finished. Early the next day, the *griot* and his family pack up their belongings and return to the road.

These *griots* were walking encyclopedias of local history, and they knew details about people's lives that would have shocked many; yet they could not imagine the shattering changes that would sweep across West Africa, carrying millions of them to a land impossibly far away, a land with bizarre and inscrutable customs. As the slave ships patrolled the coastal waters, and the slavers traveled further and further inland to gather human cattle, many *griots* were taken captive and chained up in the fetid holds of the slave ships bound for the

New World. Many Africans died on these voyages, and some took their own lives by jumping into the sea, rather than endure the indignities that awaited them.

Those who survived the voyage arrived on foreign soil with only two things: their basic human dignity and the cultural traditions that reaffirmed it, both of which the Americans fought hard to wipe out. But the slavers would have had to literally cut out the tongues of the Africans to do that, because the key to the Africans' roots was largely contained in their songs. As the slaves sung and hollered, digging in the vast cotton tracts of the American South, they were simultaneously redigging ancient roots, remembering bloodlines and relinking themselves to a racial soul with heart cries of living poetry. Some may even have managed to carry along their *halams*, for it is generally believed that the American banjo is a direct descendant of this African instrument. In any case, the *griots* and other musicians would certainly have fashioned themselves new instruments the first chance they got after landing on foreign soil. Music was not only essential to all of their social and religious rituals, it was literally inseparable from life as they knew it.

The Beat Lives On . . .

> My music has a little bit of a spiritual taste, but it's also
> primitive. I play the guitar as if I was playing drums.
> —Bo Diddley[8]

The other prevalent musical style of West Africa that migrated across the Atlantic was polyrhythmic drumming, which was more prevalent in the tribes of the tropical rain forest. When Africans get together to drum and dance all night long they are not simply having a good

time (although they are not adverse to that either); they are inten-
tionally inviting the *loas*, the gods, to enter into this world and possess their bodies. Spirit possession is a highly important aspect of
African religions, and has survived intact in Voudun, Santeria and
other faiths across North and South America. In fact, the African
predilection for possession seeped into many American Christian
churches, especially in the South. Such congregations as the
Pentecostals, the Holy Rollers and others who speak in tongues and
roll around on the floor quivering in ecstasy have much more in common with so called pagan religions than they might like to believe.

For Africans, spirit possession is not solely a personal event. By
allowing a deity to take over one's body, one performs an important
function for the community. Messages from the gods are communicated through possession of their human servants, who need to have
strong personalities able to withstand the intense spiritual energy
coursing through their bodies, as well as the ability to let go and surrender to its movement. Dancing to the drums was the way that one
invited the spirits to inhabit the body. A male or female god could
take over a dancer of either sex, and the god could be recognized by
certain signs that were known to everyone in the tribe. Spirit possession is the *raison d'etre* of these rituals.

Drumming was not only essential to keep everyone dancing; specific drum patterns were used to call down specific gods, and if these
patterns were lost, the ritual literally could not happen.[9] The drummers were absolutely crucial; the right beat could open a big door
into the unseen worlds, while a mediocre one could fail to call down
any heavenly participants. This is why, in African music, rhythm is
everything. The dancers would face the drummers, because within
the drums they would hear the voice of the gods. An old African saying tells us that, "The Spirit will not descend without song."[10] This
is true in all the musical traditions of West Africa that have influ-

enced American music, including that of the *griots* and of the tribes who favor polyrhythmic drumming. Religious expression was simply unthinkable without music, and musical aptitude was not valued for its own sake, but as a potent tool for moving energy in a way that allowed for spiritual experience. This is why the Africans say that, "A village without music is a dead place."

At the time that the slave trade got underway in Africa in the 1500s, two types of musical culture existed: the Islamic-influenced music of Northwest Africa that favored stringed instruments, solo singing and richly ornamented melodies; and the drum-centered music of Central Africa, which focused heavily on polyrhythms, dancing and group singing (possibly the melodies were less complex simply to allow large groups of people to sing together in tune). Risking gross oversimplification, we could say that the former had complex melodies while the latter had complex rhythms. Hundreds of years later, when these two styles were mixed together and combined with the third ingredient—Western harmonic theory—the result would create the most cataclysmic shift of musical style the Western world had ever heard.

When the slaves arrived in the New World they first stopped in the Caribbean. The ones who were more acclimated to the tropical Caribbean heat stayed there, while the Africans from the dryer northern climates were sent to the American continent.[11] Thus, the Africans first deposited on American soil were from the Islam-influenced cultures of the *griots* from the coastal nations now called Senegal and The Gambia. Climates in these regions more closely approximated that of the South. The first tribes who arrived there probably planted the seeds for the growth of this new African American culture, dominating those tribes who came later. One of these original tribes, the Wolof, contributed many words to the lexicon of American musicians, including "dig," "jive," "funk" and "hip cat."[12]

Muslims were certainly known on the plantations, and they were often used to keep records, some of which were written in Arabic.[13] Elements of Islamic religion survived as well. There was a type of dance called a ring shout, where a group of people would gather in a circle, dancing clockwise and singing. Dr. Lorenzo Turner believes that the term "shout" actually derives from the Arabic *saut*, which means "to walk around the Kaaba," the sacred stone inside Mecca to which Muslims from all over the world make pilgrimage.[14] Since there was no chance of these transported Muslims making the official holy pilgrimage, they had to do the next best thing: invent their own rituals to compensate for this loss. In fact, just about all early African American music is imbued with this deep sense of loss; their songs burst forth from a terrible heartache, a yearning to recreate a living, nurturing, spiritual culture that had been almost decimated by their forced exodus.

The survival of the *griot* tradition was favored for another reason: drumming was forbidden on the southern plantations because the white landlords knew that the slaves could send messages through their "talking" drums and possibly organize a rebellion in that way. Also, they feared the strange power drumming seemed to unleash in the slave—a power full of dark magic and raw sexuality. So while the sound of African drumming all but died out during the slave era (saved only by the Voodoo drumming of New Orleans), stringed instruments were allowed to survive. (After the African inspired banjo, the two most popular instruments among black songsters were the guitar and the fiddle, both of Middle-East origin.) This means that the *griots* would have had a much easier time adapting to local musical styles.

In contrast to the music of the drum dominated tribes of the coastal regions, the music of the savan-

nah Sudanic regions appears to have been of a kind
that would have accorded well with the Scottish and
English folk forms and been accepted enough to have
survived among the slaves.

— Paul Oliver, *Savannah Syncopators*
African Retentions in the Blues.[15]

Akin to the European Gypsies, blacks in early America would
quickly learn Euro-American songs and adapt them to their own
rhythmic and harmonic sensibilities, which would sometimes render
the songs nearly unrecognizable to the ears of whites. This was especially true of vocal music (the only instrument most slaves had access
to was their own voice), which was transformed from a linear
Western scale into an African one, composed of bizarre (to the
untrained ear) microtonal quavers, shivers and shimmies. In fact,
many "educated" people of the time, including musicologists, were
convinced that the African-descended slaves were ignorant about
music because they insisted on flatting the thirds and sevenths, and
generally ignored all the rules of Western musical composition. It
was only later that black song styles were recognized for what they
were, a relic of a culture at least as rich and complex as the European.

B l u e   N o t e s

The music of Senegal has unmistakable Arabic strains.
Because of Senegal's many centuries of contact with the Berber
and Arab cultures north of the desert, the vocal music tends to
reflect the Middle East's predilection for long, tortuous melody
lines. And there's a fondness for solo singing, which is relatively
unusual in most African music.

— Robert Palmer, *Deep Blues*[16]

Akin to Senegalese music, blues scales achieve a mood of longing that is noticeably absent in other African music. Paul Oliver, in his book *Savannah Syncopators*, has identified the mechanics of this musical acculturation from Islam to West Africa to the blues. But one must listen and *feel* into the music to actually substantiate his theories. In one song, for instance, a singer accompanies himself on a one-string bowed fiddle called a *gogue*. The *gogue* plays the same riff throughout with small variations. It's a fast little riff repeatedly coming to an abrupt halt on a minor third—not just any minor third, but a strikingly "blue" minor third. The first time I heard this note in the piece, the whole Delta tradition came flooding in. That note ripped into my soul, spelling dissatisfaction and frustrated desire.

Noted musicologists have traced these Arabic roots of the blues when they found that "Indo-Pakistani music is divided into six principle modes, three of which . . . are nothing but the blues scale."[17] Actually, the blues scale behaves more like an Indian *raga* than a Western scale: while a scale is simply a series of notes, a *raga* is imbued with a strong sense of mood that is implied by subtle variations and bends in the notes as one ascends and descends the scale.*

I remember the first time I found one of these blue notes while playing slide guitar: it was like a revelation. Suddenly I realized that there was a note *between* the points which I had been taught all my musical life were *the only notes in existence;* it was a little bit beyond the minor third, about a third of the way to the major third. This note, impossible to hit without using a slide or bending the string, would be pronounced incorrect in most school music programs, but it sounded absolutely perfect in the context of the blues. It was as if a

---

*That the blues scale is more than a lifeless series of notes which cannot simply be parroted by anyone is shown by the treatment given to it by many heavy metal groups, which manage to make the same six notes say very different things than blues players.

shade of emotion that had been missing from my life suddenly appeared in that moment, like discovering a brand new color.

Deborah has also experienced these notes while singing. When Shri was starting out, she remembers spending a lot of time emulating her favorite blues singers,

> . . . trying to find the notes, to resonate exactly with the notes I was hearing. When I would hit the right note I would always know because I would drop down inside myself into a whole other world of experience. When you can exactly reproduce what Muddy Waters or Magic Sam was doing it's like taking a drug. Those notes can't be written on a page.

It is fascinating to consider that the Western scale system has a certain capacity to deliver a variety of moods and emotions, but that other scale systems, by adding notes that did not previously exist in our awareness, may also be communicating subtleties of feelings hitherto ignored by our culture. So the intrusion of the strange blue notes into American music have their emotional correlate—those bent notes are actually leading us into what Deborah calls ". . . a whole other world of experience."

The frequent bending of notes that is so common in the blues is integral to Arabic music, while it appears infrequently in other African musical styles:

> . . . the practice of embellishment and . . . of fluctuations and "bends" in the notes becomes steadily more marked as one moves. . . [North] . . . through the savannah regions to the desert. Perhaps it is the Arabic influence that determines this. . . Certainly the ornamentation

of the Tuarego [a tribe of the Saharan desert] reaches a
degree of enrichment that exceeds any in the blues and
comes very close to that of... flamenco.

—Paul Oliver[18]

These Arabic embellishments at first sound strange to Western
ears, just as the early music of the slaves did. Instead of being con-
fined to the seven-rung ladder of the Western scale, the vocalist plays
with the notes, jumping and sliding in between them, allowing the
feeling to dictate the technique. It's the freedom of suddenly being
able to play all the notes in between the keys of a piano—it looks
like there are a lot of notes on a piano keyboard (the ultimate instrument of Western music), but in some ways it actually leaves out more
possibility than it provides. With certain singers, the space between
"C" and "C-sharp" can contain worlds of feeling and nuance. How
one gets to the note is just as important as the note itself. Often, a
blues singer doesn't quite get there but keeps falling short, and the
note hangs there in the air, or gets caught in one's throat—it never
resolves like it should, but lingers on in a limbo of thwarted hopes
and desperate dreams. The sometimes unbearable tension these notes
create inside the listener mirrors a life of unbearable ironies.

Muslim Blues

Like the singers of the black churches and honkytonks, "Muslim
singers ornament their lines with short, microtonal shakes."[19] The
fact is that these "microtonal shakes" and ornate vocal embellishments cannot be found either in the early folk music of America, nor
in the dense rain forests of Africa. That leaves the Arabic-inspired
African music of the savannah as the only possible source for this
essential vocal technique of the blues.

Many books have touched on this Arabic connection to the blues, and a few, most notably Oliver's *Savannah Syncopators* and Samuel Charters' *The Roots of the Blues*, have explored it more deeply. John Storm Roberts explodes our myth of "pure" African music when he says:

> Africa has always been in contact with other parts of the world . . . North Africa was an area of myriad musical influences. It had heard Phoenician, Greek, Roman, and Byzantine music before falling to invaders who brought an Arabic music containing elements of Coptic, Syrian, Egyptian and Persian music, and even, some think, Indian. Arabic Music—in its part African Moorish form—is a highly important link between the musical worlds of Europe, West Africa, and parts of the New World.[20]

Alan Lomax also finds a connection between Africa and the East:

> . . . West Africa—the seat of the slave trade—has long had a solo string-accompanied bardic tradition, with evident connections to the Moslem, the Mediterranean, and ultimately the Asian world.[21]

It was this Eastern-influenced bardic tradition that was to transform itself into what we know today as the blues. Perhaps the seeds of the Islamic musical traditions were able to bear fruit on the American continent because the mood of longing that Middle-Eastern music typically inspires—with its minor keys and long, tortured vocal lines—perfectly fit the mood in which the slaves found and needed to express themselves.

There is a long tradition of love poetry in the Islamic world, and these poems are very often set to music. The general mood of these songs is that of longing for the beloved. The lyrics can be mundane or spiritual, but usually they skillfully bridge both worlds. The words dance around the striking features of the man or woman in question, caressing their object of love with potent phrases of desire. Yet at the same time they describe a mood of longing that goes beyond the physical; the human lover becomes a doorway to the Divine. And in that recognition of spiritual perfection in a human being, the highest path is to give up ever consummating that love, but instead to rest in a perpetual state of unrequited love, to allow the fire to grow and grow until it consumes one totally in its heat and brightness. This is the recurrent theme of much Arabic music, and this is the mood that it often engenders in its listeners.

Here was a mood with which the displaced Africans were quite familiar. Their litanies of loss spilled forth from their lips as inspired songs of prayer. Their love for their homeland would forever remain unrequited.

P r e a c h i n ' T h e   B l u e s

'Course, you know a spiritual song can get
closer to me than the blues. Sometimes . . .
—"Mississippi" Fred McDowell

One of my fondest memories of touring France with Shri is driving along the lush orchards of Provence, through endless fields of perfect peaches and apricots. Often we would stop at a roadside stand and buy a crate of peaches for the equivalent of just a few dollars. Those peaches were more luscious than chocolate! We could polish off an entire box within twenty-four hours.

On one peach-eating journey we made our way to Les Mées, a tiny town in the heart of Provence. Winding our way into hills richly laden with olive trees, we found the town nestled between a meandering river and a small mountain that shoots up only several hundred yards from the shore of the river. Just above the old village houses, a couple of dozen gigantic stones are lined up like soldiers along the side of the mountain. They're called *Les Penitents*, and the villagers told us a story about them.

Long ago, in a time when the region was ruled by Muslims, there was a Christian monastery at Les Mées. The ruler of the region had many women brought from the East to be his wives. When they arrived, they had to walk through the town to get to his castle, and of course everyone, including the monks, came out to see these exotic dark-skinned women in their ornate silk clothes. The abbot of the monastery noticed that some of the monks were lusting after these Eastern women, so to punish the monks for their sin he changed them into stones, and there they still remain, silently casting the umbrage of their sin upon the townspeople. No matter where we found ourselves as we wandered through the narrow, labyrinthine streets of the village, we had only to look up to be reminded of their foreboding presence. The people here seemed a little suspicious of strangers, and now I knew why: this was a town with a past, and I could feel it hanging on.

We pulled up to the address we were given for our venue to find that obviously a mistake had been made—our directions had led us to the great wooden doors of an old church which looked like it would fall apart at the mere suggestion of loud music. After hearing the story of *Les Penitents*, I certainly didn't want to mess with the religious authorities in this town. But, after some investigation, it turned out that we were in fact in the right place for our gig.

The moment I walked into the building and looked up at the vaulted ceiling a hundred feet above me, the reality hit. We were to set up the drums right in front of the altar, upon which was an ornate frontispiece of Jesus and the twelve apostles at the Last Supper. I was thrilled. The humor of the situation was so undeniably rich: after twelve years of suffocating Catholic school, what better way to heal my past than to bring the passion and energy of what I love to do right up on the altar?

During sound check I kept turning about, gazing at all the familiar statues: Christ calling his flock with his arms outstretched, offering salvation; Mary tenderly holding the infant Jesus; the solemn presence of the Crucifix. Images of our wildest gigs came to me, transposed onto this scene. Maybe God does have a sense of humor after all, I mused.

When we returned after dinner, the pews were filled with people dressed in their Sunday best. Seeing such an intent audience made us a little nervous, because we knew all the other shows they had witnessed here were of classical music. What were they expecting from us?

Since we didn't want to blow out the crowd in this subdued setting, we decided to play a slow, quiet set. Yet we couldn't fill two hours with mellow blues, so every three or four songs we would get a little rowdy. The music sent swelling waves of sensuousness into the body of the church, creating a vibration that had probably never been felt in this place before. The lyrics of our songs certainly brought up ideas that were never before considered from this pulpit:

> I watch you playin'
> With all the other girls
> And I'd like you to play
> With a few of my curls
> Will you come on over
> To my back yard
> Got a job for you honey
> Though it might be hard
>
> Yes love me darlin'
> And love me true
> Got a whole lot of sugar
> That is meant for you

Yes love me baby
And love me right
Treat me to your candy
Each and every night.[1]

I found it pretty funny to see these conservatively dressed people sitting in church, their feet tapping, heads bobbing and bodies swaying in those severe wooden pews. Thinking back, I wonder what they would have done if we had tried to get them out of those pews and into the aisles dancing, just like those southern revival meetings, where practically anything went if it was in the name of the Lord. But as much as I'd like to say so, nothing quite like that happened.

For the most part, the crowd sat in rapt attention—we all reveled in the mood of awe and quiet devotion that permeated the air, and I was thrilled to hear some of our lyrics as if for the first time. This was our most soothing, peaceful gig ever. Most touching for me perhaps is a song called *Driftin'*, which like many of our pieces raises the love between man and woman to enraptured, holy heights.

Driftin' on the clouds of delight
Simply driftin', under your touch
Oh when you found me
I was so hard to be kissed
But you persisted
And I thank you so much

Now I am driftin', lost in the mood
Floating from your love
Oh how you moved me
How you turned me around
Pulled me from the bottom

To the Heavens above

Driftin', with no thoughts in my mind
Driftin' possessed by you
Glad to be set free
From my hard core heart
What a lovely obsession
You have chained me to

Driftin' in the sun of your eyes
Darlin' how could you know
I was so completely lost
And you knew it too
And you saved me
Took me in tow[2]

The words of this prayerful song echoed in the huge cathedral, creating an eerie other-worldly sound, and I noticed many of the faces in the audience had tears streaming down. What a perfect place to play this song, I thought; such a tender and intimate confession of the love that is possible between man and woman. I felt like a tiny victory had been made, a small but tangible healing of the long-standing societal wound created by a worn-out theology that convinced us that sex was closer to sin that salvation—a belief that still poisons many of our institutions.

If Shri had ever preached the blues, that was the night. In an ancient, broken down church, the sermon that night was given by a soul stirrin' mama named Deborah Auletta, and she let people know that God didn't just live in the sky. At any moment, he could bridge the distance of a million miles, burning into their lives on the wings of love, turning man and woman into god and goddess, turning these fecund Provence fields into an earthly paradise. Now that was a soul satisfyin' gig!

"Grandma, Did Rock and Roll Really Begin in Church?"

These days church does not provide the kind of community focal point that it used to. In the South, before blacks won a political voice, the church was the only place where they could safely express their deepest sorrows. A chorus of voices might thunder through a ramshackle church, threatening to shake and jangle it to the ground with the raw force of nature itself. A mighty sound would arise from the breasts of the singers as they called out in anguish for the Lord's help. The repeated phrases and clapping roared like a powerful locomotive, a spiritual train direct to Jesus. Alan Lomax, one of a handful of white people privy to these powerful and intimate gatherings, described a typical Delta church service:

> The voices of the preacher and the convention blended in a sound that shook the building. Tears streamed down many faces . . . I felt witness to things I knew little about, feelings that were beyond my comprehension. My heart had struck a depth of sorrow and hurt such as I had never imagined. I began to see what a painful road I was to travel in the land where the blues began.[3]
>
> I confess that I blacked out at times and did not attend to all that happened . . . It was too intense, too pain-filled . . . the agony was real . . .[4]

But there was a beauty to these services as well; the longing of the congregation reached toward unearthly heights of joy.

"Rocking" (as in "rocking and rolling") began in the black churches. One was rocked by the Holy Spirit, a kind of spiritual ecstasy. The word summons images of being rocked in the arms of a mother, as well as of the rhythms of sexual embrace, as in "rock me all night long." In the black church, being rocked meant being surrendered to a higher force, allowing it to sweep through the participants' bodies like a storm and wipe away their sins, their troubles and their grief, so that the Holy Spirit was made visible. The fact that African American culture had the same word, "rocking," for sex and spiritual experience sums up how very different it was from the Western culture that surrounded it.

All these examples of rocking—motherly protection, spiritual surrender and sexual abandon—relate to the feminine principle. In my view, being rocked was to put oneself in the hands of the Mother Goddess, Shakti, the prime mover of sexual energy, the Muse of all muses, the ruler of birth and death. While God resided upstairs in an unreachable heaven, the Goddess played with us right here on earth.

The celebration of human goodness radiantly overflowed from these services, washing over the participants like a baptism of sound. The mystery of the power of the human voice invoked awe, as each singer added his or her own spontaneous "unschooled" variations seemingly randomly, all somehow commingling in miraculous harmony. These notes secretly spelled out the word *Joy*, inscribing itself on the heart of anyone in need who would listen openly. The voices wove through the church, connecting all in a patchwork quilt of revelatory good feeling. The spontaneous and pure use of voice for worship arose from the need to express love for the Creator and his creation—this was the height of artistic expression, where art ended and some bigger process took over.

Buddy Guy described his early experience in church, which remains with him to this day as he wails the blues on his guitar:

> Every time my mama would walk into church, she'd start cryin'. This is the thing I feel when I play—the Baptist comin' out of me, 'cause I seen it done a lot of times in the Black church. People get up, and they just get to shakin'; and they scream loud . . . bringing it from inside 'til my chill runs out my eyes. They say that's the spirit comin' out of you.[5]

This kind of ecstatic surrender to the feminine principle is a mainstay of African worship, and it never entirely died out in the religious practice of most African Americans. We all get a taste of it in the music that arose out of these religious rituals.

The worship of the Euro-American Protestants of the same time period was another story. This quote by a minister in the nineteenth century makes the point:

> The public worship of God should be conducted with reverence and stillness on the part of the congregation; nor should the minister . . . encourage demonstrations of approbation or disapprobation, or exclamations, or response, or noises, or outcries of any kind during the progress of divine worship; nor boisterous singing. . .[6]

Needless to say, black worship changed things.

The Transformation of a Creed

The God spoken about in the black songs is not the same one in the white songs . . . though the words might look the same. But it is a different quality of energy they summon.

—Stephen Cone[7]

Rock! Oh—rock in this weary land!

—Traditional black spiritual[8]

The first place where whites and blacks in America got together to make music was in church. Of course, for the Anglo-Saxons, music was not the purpose for these meetings, but only served to convey certain points. For the blacks, however, music itself was an act of worship. These two modes of worship—the emotionally reserved services of post-Puritan Protestantism, and the intensely personal and passionate black religious experience—influenced each other irrevocably.

At first, blacks were reticent to give up their traditional religious practices and participate in Christianity. But the Great Awakening, the nineteenth century religious movement that encouraged ecstatic body-oriented participation, quickly drew in large numbers of African Americans. Charismatic preachers roamed the countryside, holding spontaneous revival meetings in huge tents or in open fields. This was a place where blacks could practice religion in familiar ways. Cries and groans filled the air as men and women ". . . leaped out of their seats, screamed, jerked, shouted, fell into convulsions, spoke in tongues, and engaged in holy convulsions."[9] Music helped to create this highly charged atmosphere. The white congregation enjoyed the singing of the blacks, and would sometimes remain silent just to listen more intently.

Black musical sensibilities were really beginning to permeate the consciousness of white America. Some church leaders didn't like the singing of the blacks; they felt that they distorted the sense and meaning of the church songs with their frightening wails and moans. But there were others who felt the opposite, that the fevered pitch of feeling that was being injected into the music was uncovering the true and essential message hidden inside.

African Americans took what the Christian hymn books had to offer and made it completely their own. They immediately identified with the lost tribe of the Israelites, who, like the Africans, were conquered by another tribe and wandered in the land of their enemies for many years, searching for the land of Canaan. The African Americans' burning need to recreate and maintain their traditions led them to transform traditional Protestant hymns in order to reflect their own experience: Canaan became equated with Canada, a land without slavery, and the concept of spiritual freedom was a convenient guise for singing about freedom from slavery. And just as the songs and poetry of a tiny tribe in the Palestinian desert spread further than their dreams could comprehend, so too did those early spirituals and blues songs. Born in broken down shacks, lost within the endless rows of cotton and seemingly destined for obscurity, the songs of these poor, illiterate men and women transformed the way America (and the world) looked at music. Ironically, though the people themselves wielded almost no power to change a nation that desperately needed changing, their blues would carry forth their spirit— timeless, protean and totally infectious.

Bluesmen and Preachers

I swear to God, I've got to preach these gospel blues.
—Son House, *Preachin' the Blues*

From the beginning, the blues was a direct outgrowth of the black religious experience. Almost all the great seminal figures in the blues had strong connections to the black church. They could sing any number of old-time spirituals with as much facility and conviction as they brought to their blues songs. Robert Johnson's mother would berate him about playing the devil's music, but when he took out his harmonica and started blowing familiar spirituals she would forget her opposition to his wayward lifestyle and "get happy," singing along.

The split which eventually arose between the church and the blues singers was not created by the bluesmen and women, but by the church, which was influenced by Western notions of sin and propriety. The church did not have room for aspects of African religious life that were hitherto integral parts of community ritual: celebration of the body through dancing, and the invitation of the spirits into *this* world. There was an element of sensual abandon, of allowing uncontrollable chthonic forces their play, which was categorically out of bounds. The innocent, open and playful relationship with eroticism that characterizes the blues was barred from expression in this new kind of worship. And in the juke joints, blues singers had to be careful about breaking into spiritual numbers—singing the blues was one thing, but mixing the music of the devil with the songs of the Lord was unthinkable.

By and large, the black church assumed the Western-European attitude that surrounded them: that there was a fundamental moral difference between the soul and the flesh, and if you wanted to save

Eddie "Son" House: spiritual father of the blues.

your soul then you best not play around too much with the body. From there, it was a small step to the belief that the body itself and all its attendant feelings were inherently sinful. So the blues, savoring the erotic, and giving a voice to violent rage and inconsolable grief that had been choked back for so long, was branded the "devil's music."

Some blues musicians joked that if their music was paving the road to hell, they figured it was probably a whole lot more fun there anyway, because there wasn't any whiskey, women or gambling in heaven. Underneath the lighthearted façade, however, was often a deeply troubled artist who felt called to the blues life (as a preacher is called to a life in the church), yet was often looked upon with scorn by his own people.

Ironically, both blues artists and preachers were moved by the same desire to bring healing and wholeness into themselves and into the lives of their community, but when it came to the method of healing, they did not see eye to eye. They were now laboring under the weight of the Western body/mind split that was seeping into their culture.

As we noted earlier, African religion propitiates different aspects of Divinity depending on the situation. Thus, the role of the black preacher was solely concerned with these larger issues of faith and with propitiating the supreme god for his help, while the bluesman was left with the task of addressing the day-to-day concerns like marital problems and the struggle to earn a living. The preacher and the bluesman were performing different functions, which, in ancient tribal cultures, used to be the domain of one person—the shaman.

From the Church to the Juke Joint

Inspired performers constantly blurred the line between preaching and entertainment. One Saturday night, Son House, apparently forgetting where he was, got up on a table to preach in the middle of a juke joint. And Charlie Patton, known as the father of the Delta blues and House's mentor, recorded numerous spirituals and sermons as well as blues, and spent his last days preaching. While many members of the religious community sermonized that the blues was anathema to the souls of upstanding church-going men and women, people like Patton couldn't seem to put down either the life of the bluesman or the preacher. I think the tension created by this dilemma ate away at the spirits of many of the great early bluesmen, and was partly responsible for their untimely deaths, including Patton's, whose life of hard drinking caught up with him in his forties.

The list of great bluesmen who have dabbled in preaching, or at least seriously considered it, includes Son House, Muddy Waters, Blind Willie McTell and Charlie Patton. An impressive list! Leafing through an encyclopedia of the blues, one phrase gets repeated more than any other: "Began singing in church." There are numerous examples of artists crossing over to the church in other genres as well, including Little Richard and Jerry Lee Lewis in rock and roll, and Aretha Franklin and Al Green in soul music. The interest in spirituality of these vital and groundbreaking performers would often create severe moral and creative dilemmas in their lives; they had an intense, unrelenting calling to give something to others, yet they did not know how, for their message involved both the holy shouts of the church and the lowdown moans of the juke joints.

Son House

Son House had done some preaching as a young man, but he could not keep away from the blues. At one point his father told him that he shouldn't "hold God in one hand and the devil in the other," so he had to make a decision. He chose the blues, but mysteriously drifted away from it only to be discovered a quarter century later, barely remembering many of his old songs. Alan Lomax described Son House's fire-and-brimstone blues in this famous passage:

> Son House, [was] a man transformed, no longer the quiet, affable person I had met, but possessed by the song, as Gypsies in Spain are possessed, gone blind with music and poetry. "Hitch up my black pony, saddle up my bay mare," he sang, his words conjuring up nights of coupling in the tropical heat of Mississippi. His voice, guttural and hoarse with passion, ripping apart the surface of the music like his tractor-driven plow ripped apart the wet black earth in the springtime, making the sap of the earth song run . . . with him the sorrow of the blues was not tentative, or retiring, or ironic. Son's whole body wept, as with eyes closed, the tendons in his powerful neck standing out with the violence of his feeling and his brown face flushing.[10]

His most famous song, *Preachin' the Blues*, perfectly captures the spiritual dilemma in which many blues singers found themselves—needing the salvific spirit of God and the community of believers, yet unable to give up their devotion to the world of women, whiskey and music.

> Oh, I'm gonna get me religion, I'm gonna join
>   the Baptist Church
> Oh, I'm gonna get me religion, I'm gonna join

the Baptist Church
I'm gonna be a Baptist preacher, and I sure won't
    have to work

Oh, in my room, I bowed down to pray
Oh—I was in my room, I bowed down to pray
Then the blues came 'long and they blowed
    my spirit away

Oh, I have religion on this very day
Oh, I have religion on this very day
But the womens and whiskey, well they would not
    let me pray.

Oh, I wish I had me a heaven of my own
Yeahh . . . a heaven of my own
Well I'd give all my women a long long happy home

Oh, I got to stay on the job, I ain't got no time to
    lose
Yeahh . . . I ain't got no time to lose
I swear to God, I've got to preach these gospel blues
    (Great God amighty)

Oh, I'm gonna preach these blues now and choose
    my seat and set down
Oh, I'm gonna preach these blues now and choose
    my seat and set down
When the spirit comes sisters, I want you to jump
    straight up and down.[11]

—Son House

Son House really did preach his blues! The original recording is filled with such ferocious conviction that after listening to it you don't know if you want to run out and join the church or get smashed at the nearest bar. And apparently neither did Son House.

The first verse of the song takes a pretty clear swipe at the preachers, whom many considered lazy and philandering. One of the many preacher jokes current at the time summed up the situation. One night during his sermon, the preacher asked all the people in the congregation who loved the Lord more than they loved sinning to sit on one side of the aisle, and all the people who loved whiskey and philandering more than the Lord to sit on the other. After all had moved to their respective seats, one man remained standing in the center of aisle. The preacher asked him what he was doing there, to which the man replied that as much as he worshipped the Lord with all his heart and soul, he was also completely devoted to women and whiskey. He loved both equally! The preacher beamed with delight and shouted, "Son, come right up here to the pulpit. I believe you been called to preach!" Underneath this ribald humor simmers the spirit/body split that tore apart the African worldview and infected blacks with the same disease of guilt and shame around sexuality that has plagued Western society for so long.*

The next two verses are nearly identical in describing an urge toward religion that was thwarted in various ways, first by "the blues" and then by "womens and whiskey." We've covered the women and

* The role of the bluesman in African American culture is similar to that of the sacred clown in some Native American tribes. These clowns actually perform a respected ritual function by purposefully ridiculing the priests and acting in profane and crass ways. They make sure that people don't take things so seriously that they lose their sense of humor, which they consider a vital part of life. The black preacher also had his sacred clown in the bluesman, albeit one that he didn't appreciate too much.

whiskey dilemma, but why would the blues stop Son House from praying? (I take it here that by "the blues" he means not the music but the condition of soul.) He wanted to pray, but somehow the prayers of the church were not amenable to his spirit. The blues blew away his spirit to pray, so all he could do was sing out his blues. When he says, "I swear to God, I've got to preach these gospel blues (Great God amighty)," there is no doubt that he is serious about his mission, even though it doesn't fit into any of the prescribed ways for a man to live his life. Son House was obviously a man who felt called to preach, yet he could not reconcile himself with the restrictive lifestyle that befell Christian preachers. He also had other arguments with organized religion.

> Yeah, it ain't no heaven now and it
> ain't no burnin' hell
> Said where I'm goin' when I die,
> can't nobody tell
> —Son House, *My Black Mama*

Yet in the same song, Son House calls on the Lord, presumably to repair a relationship jeopardized by his alcohol enflamed temper:

> Oh, Lord have mercy on my wicked soul
> I wouldn't mistreat you baby, for my weight in gold
> Oh, Lord have mercy on my wicked soul
> Mmmm mmmm mmmm mmmm

Gripped in an unresolvable spiritual dilemma, Son House ends the verse moaning and groaning his blues away.

Mississippi Fred

Mississippi Fred McDowell was born in 1904 in Rossville, Tennessee, but didn't make his first recording until 1959. His music, more than any other blues music I know, obliterates the so-called line between the blues and spirituals. Fred shifted from one to the other and back again with such grace and fluidity that one hardly noticed how unusual it was to do that. Whether he was singing about his Lord Jesus with heartfelt gladness or crying out the bitter pain of lost love, Fred's incredible openness and generosity fills each song with an unforgettable mood of human tenderness. Hearing Fred sing *Shake it on Down* side by side with *Jesus is on the Main Line*, we wonder what the fuss was all about anyway. His songs convey a wide palette of moods, but there is nothing in either his spirituals or his blues that negates the spirit of the other. As he says, "It's just like if you're going to pray, and mean it . . . songs should tell the truth."[12]

Fred was not a typical juke joint bluesman. He played his music at parties for friends around Como, a small town in the hill country of Mississippi, and every Sunday he would join his wife, relatives and friends at the Hunter Chapel, singing spirituals and providing slide guitar accompaniment. The area around Como was home to a unique musical tradition that still bore close parallels with African music: the fife and drum tradition, the only drum-based African music to survive on the American continent besides the Voodoo drumming of New Orleans. The blues that comes out of this area has hard driving, rich rhythms, often with no chord changes at all. Possibly, it was this strong presence of African music in this area of Mississippi that allowed Fred and others to see the close parallels between the blues and spirituals, rather than drawing rigid boundaries between them.

Fred stated with conviction that the blues issued directly from singing in church. He called it "confessing" religion, but it's not about telling your sins; it's about sharing faith in the Lord through song, a remembrance of the conversion, the moment when the Spirit became flesh within one's own trembling body. Fred's spirituals "rock" while his blues lift our spirit, and frequently his songs combine elements of both hard-edged blues and sweet spirituals, for while his voice is weighed down by earthly misery, his steakbone slide glides up the guitar strings, quavering in heavenly bliss. More than any guitarist I have heard, his slide playing is an extension of his voice, communicating a depth of feeling to which words could never do justice. Frequently he will sing the first half of a line and let his slide guitar finish it off, true to the African call-and-response style. Alan Lomax's words describe him best: "You feel that the underlying mood of his music is as grave as the tragic destiny of his people. Yet the dancing beat that rocked the barrelhouse all night long rolls and jangles joyously."[13]

Even today, the men and women who play this music approach with a kind of devotion normally reserved for the religious calling.

Fred McDowell singing with his wife, Annie Mae.

Recently, at a local blues club, I saw Big Jack Johnson (of The Jelly Roll Kings) laying down some great Mississippi juke joint music, attacking his guitar strings with demonic intensity and whipping the crowd into a frenzy. After his gig I got up the nerve to ask him the big question of this book, which is (for those of you who haven't guessed by now): "Do you think the blues is religious music?"

"Yes," he immediately responded. "I preach this music. I got the Bible out there in my truck." How many bluesmen have alluded to that, I wondered. He lowered his head and suddenly became quiet and thoughtful for a few moments. When he looked up there were tears in his eyes. "It's about all the sadness you ever had in your life. You play it and it makes you want to go home and ask your family for forgiveness, say 'I'm sorry for all the wrong things that I done.'"

Big Jack's sincerity was heartbreaking. The pain of the blues was so close to the surface with this man. At this moment the rest of the room disappeared and there was just he and I sitting there at the corner of the bar. He continued: "You see, God wants you, but the devil wants you too. Everything wants you. The earth wants you, wants to swallow you up. . . the sea wants you, that's what makes people drown. The wind wants you when it howls. . . and don't forget God wants you and the devil wants you. The choice is up to you."[14]

I felt that he and others of his generation had somehow retained a morsel of ancient wisdom, handed down over generations through stories, myths and music. I had always felt this hidden kernel of spirituality at the core of this music, and I had suspected that those who made the music had kept it secret on purpose. After all, for the black American slaves and their descendants, the African way of life had been all but decimated in the last several hundred years. Why would they want to give away what little of their cultural heritage they had managed to hold onto to a culture which had so far proven at best indifferent and patronizing, and at worst callous and cruel?

The Transcendence of Hopelessness

The early blues players were performing an important need with their happy/sad music, confronting the harsh realities of this life head on, without promise of redemption in the next. While the spirituals were hopeful, the blues preached a kind of transcendent hopelessness. And as blues players and lovers often testify, there is another kind of release in simply accepting whatever life gives. When all hope is abandoned, it is possible to suddenly connect to the moment like never before. When I give up hope in this way, actions and feelings become more real, my clinging to the past and fears of the future less so. I am released from my illusion that someone or someplace else is going to make it all better, or that I am not ultimately responsible for my life, and alone.

Accepting "what is" is the allure of the blues. Deep down I think we all want to do this, to sink into the present reality and drop the huge weight of judgments, expectations and fantasies based on the past. Even if we believe it is terrible to be unhappy, there can be tremendous relief in accepting our condition. And it is often easier than trying to change it. The blues says, "Fuck it! I know what life is and I'm gonna sing about it and have a good time anyway."

Blues and gospel are like twin sisters who were separated at an early age: they may have gone different ways, but each will always contain a part of the other. Gospel can still get down and dirty, and blues can lift up the heaviest souls. It's all a matter of the starting point. Gospel starts with the spirit, blues with the "down in the dirt" reality. The blues finally captured the nation's attention because we had our head up our ass. Americans needed to drop false hope and hear about the world right in front of their noses and the one right underneath their breastbone and the one between their legs. We needed something to take us out of our head and into our heart, our loins and our feet.

Chapter 4

The Shaman:
The Original Hoochie
Coochie Man

Touring with Shri can be an explosive situation sometimes. The chemistry of each participant combines to form a mixture that bubbles and seethes with an intensity that is hard to control. This volatility is a double-edged sword. It can be channeled into our musical work together and produce a visible electricity of happiness, healing and love within the group, which radiates out to those around us; or it can stoke the fire of our neurotic tendencies, which produces chilling and ugly behaviors of control, fear, manipulation and withdrawal. The music is one of the keys to channeling this energy, and we have all experienced the miracles it has produced for us.

On a sticky summer night in July, 1997, Shri needed a miracle. The rigors of the road were getting to us: we were snapping at each other viciously; some were skulking around like wounded animals; most of us were ready to walk out on the whole thing at any moment.

That night we were expecting Lee, our lyricist, to join us at the club and sing a few songs with us. Lee, who has inspired us with his lyrics for five years, strikes most people as an unassuming guy, but when he gets onstage he becomes a different person, a wildman, a trickster injecting his eccentric humor at unexpected moments. He is a master at turning up the heat in any situation and drawing out the best in all of us. On a night like this we were all looking forward to his refreshing way of seeing things, as well as his deep-felt joy and appreciation for the blues.

This gig was in a small town, along a winding road beset with sleepy quaint villages. Clouds ruled the sky as we pulled up to the club, which seemed big enough to accommodate most of the local community—half of it doubled as a café and magazine stand, and a few old men were sitting around drinking coffee and smoking, as French bluesy rock was piped in over the speakers. Evidently this club was *the* hangout spot in town. The owner was heavily into Americana—a huge poster of Easy Rider adorned the back wall of the stage, and looming above where I was to play was a cow skull covered in leather. Another small showroom featured a shiny Harley Davidson surrounded by a wall of old electric guitars. The whole place had a kind of sacred aura about it.

After a long, sumptuous French country meal we came back to the club ready to play, somewhat softened up by the French hospitality. A crowd was gathering and I could already feel their strong attention on us. The first two rows of folding chairs were completely taken up with wide-eyed children, intently watching our every move. (I take it as the highest compliment whenever children groove on our music.) We had a great light show at this gig, and the hot red, blue and yellow spots combined with the warmth of the eager and curious crowd created an atmosphere of burning desire, perfect for a night of music/lovemaking.

The crowd swayed and bopped to the music, as their eyes remained glued to the band. During the third song I looked over at some friends and there standing against the wall was Lee, smiling and unobtrusive, sporting a new "House of Blues" T-shirt, on the front of which is the image of a bleeding heart encircled with a crown of thorns. His mischievous smile told me he was primed to play.

When we were warmed up, Lee joined us onstage to sing an old blues tune by Elmore James, called, strangely enough, *My Bleeding Heart*. When Lee dives into the blues he goes deep, unleashing his subterranean voice on the unsuspecting crowd with total abandon. He growled out the words, his body slowly rocking back and forth mesmerizingly behind the beat, leaning way into his microphone as if he could pour himself into it and rush out of the speakers as pure waves of sound and fury. As he lamented, "People, people, people . . . do you know what it's like to be all alone,"[1] his body drooped almost halfway to the floor, his free arm wrapped around his torso as if he was in mortal pain.

As I watched him, the bleeding heart on his shirt brought back distant memories of a similar picture on the wall of the dining room in my childhood home—it is the Sacred Heart of Jesus. Christ rips open his chest with his hands to reveal his own heart encircled with a crown of thorns, bleeding and on fire. As a small child that picture scared me to death, but there was also something fascinating about it: in the midst of his obvious suffering, Christ's face was completely serene and compassionate. Two thousand years later, it's not a bad icon for this music. The Sacred Heart seems to be about allowing life to wound us over and over without trying to protect ourselves, simply letting that wound become an invitation for a kind of vulnerability with others beyond anything we've known before. While modern life is less about contending with suffering and more about seeking out comfort, the power of this sacred symbol is strangely resurrected for me by the blues. I believe it is an image that the collective psyche needs right now, and it is finding an opening into that psyche in this music of the brokenhearted.

And here was Lee, taking on the pain of the world through singing the blues. He turned to me, as it was time to take my solo, and groaned, "Come on Ed, make me bleed." I was momentarily stunned because he seemed dead serious, like he wanted me to stab him right there and then with the neck of my guitar, and the part of me that can't bear to have people say things that make no sense and threaten my nice neat sense of reality wanted to put down my guitar and say, "What the hell do you mean by that?!" He was going down into the pits of hell right there on stage, and he was taking as many of us with him as he could.

I have no doubt that Lee understood this song to the core, even though it came out of the harsh realities of the Mississippi Delta, while Lee grew up in the placid suburbs of New Jersey. In that moment though, Lee had completely shed the conventions of his past: he was a beggar, bereft of all human warmth and comfort, all alone in a huge, dark, threatening universe. He had become everyman's pain and suffering and despair, pure human longing, diving straight into the wound that only God could heal. The blues is about hanging out in that place, getting what it has to offer, and living to tell about it—the shamanic journey. The paradox is that we play the blues to take our blues away; we go into and through the pain, never around it. When Lee sings a song like *My Bleeding Heart*, he doesn't leave any side exits—he leads us straight into the wilderness of our psyches: dense, dark, chaotic, and definitely not sentimental.

As a group, we often refer to "the music" as having some kind of transformative power that we can tap into both as performers and as audience. A song is not some "thing," some object of art, but more like a place we can go to inside ourselves. A song can be a doorway to a particular room in the labyrinthine mansion of human experience, a room that communicates a kind of archetypal mood, a state of mind that anybody on the face of the earth could relate to. (*My Bleeding Heart* is certainly one of those songs.) That's why traditions are created and continue to provide sustenance for countless generations, because the cultural artifacts they produce (songs, dance, stories, etc.) contain powerful, universal truths. This is the answer I would give to someone who might ask why blues performers rely so much on old standards rather than coming up with original material: why mess with perfection? A good song contains a seed of truth, and a good musician brings that seed to fruition with the waters of his own passion for life.

"Make me bleed." That's something I'm still chewing on. Maybe it is myself that I must pierce, or allow to be pierced, like the heart on Lee's shirt that is completely vulnerable, ripped open to the endless ache of humanity.

The First Performers

> *The Priest or Medicine Man was the chief surviving institution the African slaves brought with them. He early appeared on the plantation and found his function as healer of the sick, the interpreter of the Unknown, the comforter of the sorrowing, the supernatural avenger of wrong and the one who rudely but picturesquely expressed the longing, disappointment and resentment of a stolen and oppressed people.*
>
> —W.E.B. Dubois[2]

The blues have always been a part of us. Ever since human beings began to wonder who they were and what their place was in this beautiful yet violent and chaotic world, there was that pain of long-ing pulsing in their chests, crying out for expression. The task of being human feels like the loneliest job on the planet, as we alone are separated from nature by this blessing and curse we call self-con-sciousness. There is a deep, primordial sadness within us, a collective pool of sorrow in the human racial memory, because we seem to have been left to figure out our place in the scheme of things by ourselves. We don't know where we come from or where we're going, and we sometimes see the majestic possibility of human life suddenly snuffed out by cruelty or chance. The earth feeds and nourishes us, provides us with shelter and clothing; yet, in an instant, she can swal-low us up with crushing indifference. The myth of expulsion from the Garden of Eden is not unique to Judaeo-Christian tradition; many cultures, including African ones, have told stories about how the original human beings, through blind chance or grave error, lost favor with God and cut themselves off from blessings. From that moment in the story we became spiritual orphans.

Where have we turned when we felt this overwhelming sensation of forlornness? Historically, this need to reconnect with our spiritu-al roots has been addressed by communal ritual. For millennia, in many cultures all night drumming, singing and dancing was the pre-ferred method of creating profound intimacy with each other and the universe. Our inner longing erupted in wails and moans, clapping and shouting, stomping and shaking, as people danced and sang with furious abandon, attempting to call the spirits down into their flesh. This mystical/musical healing ceremony was usually presided over by one who knew the terrain, who could lead his people through the dark night of the soul to healing and spiritual clarity: the shaman.

Shamanism is older than recorded history, maybe as old as humankind itself. It is found everywhere in the world, from Tibet and Siberia, to North and South America, Africa, Australia and even in the ancient Celtic culture of Europe. Anthropologists have found that the practice of shamanism is remarkably similar throughout diverse tribes. In fact, shamanism and music are two of only a few cultural traits that are so common they could be called universal.

The shaman is the prototype of what we would today call a priest, but he was much more than that: he or she was also an oracle, a medicine man or woman, a musician and a magician. Simply put, the shaman was (and still is) the go-between for his or her community and the worlds of the spirit. Just as all human beings carry within them an innate spiritual longing, so it seems that there is within human communities a need for specialists fluent in conversing with the spirit realm. Shamans are individuals who are called to this task, who have a unusual need to contact the mysterious power at the source of the universe, and who pay for this privilege by serving others with the gifts that they bring back.

How does one become a shaman? Usually, that one is marked out from the rest of the tribe by an ordeal of extraordinary suffering early in life. Many are orphaned; some get so sick that they cross the threshold of death; some undergo severe psychological dysfunction. Then a breakthrough occurs—the would-be shaman calls on the spirits of the tribe for help, and they teach him how to heal himself. By navigating through their own particular spiritual crises, shamans are invested with supernatural power; while it is not their own power, they have the ability to call it down for those in need.

If we look at the childhood of many great contemporary performers we often see this kind of severe trauma. Robert Johnson never knew his real father; in his youth he wandered about with his destitute mother from labor camps to plantations. Shortly after their early marriage his wife died in childbirth—she was only fifteen. Soon after, he left home to learn the blues and became a legend in his own time. Jimi Hendrix, who took the blues to interstellar heights, was abandoned by his mother and shipped around from home to home, never gaining a sense of family. In adulthood, he was rarely seen without his guitar, even as he cooked himself breakfast or went to the bathroom. BB King's parents separated when he was four. His mother died when he was nine and his adolescent sweetheart died when she was sixteen. For fifty years BB King has played at least three hundred nights a year, bringing the blues to millions of people all over the world. Muddy Waters lost his mother when he was three, and his father was run out of town by a lynch mob, leaving his grandmother to raise him. He left home in his late twenties, and practically invented the Chicago blues sound.

The similarities are uncanny: these people are giants—each of them irrevocably changed the way we hear and play music, and each of them underwent the kind of severe trauma that in other cultures would have marked them out as potential shamans. Through the power of music, they all sought to be reborn in the Spirit, like so many had done in the southern black churches. It is clear that the losses they suffered early in life drove them to pursue their callings with unrelenting determination. The Caribou Eskimo shaman, Igjugarjuk, said that ". . . suffering open[s] the human heart, and therefore a shaman must seek his wisdom there."[3] More than anything else, what makes a real bluesman or blueswoman is this ability to turn their suffering into wisdom, and to help others do the same.

Above all, shamanism is a practical art. It seeks tangible results for the concrete dilemmas of this world; if the shaman cannot solve the problems of his tribe, he will be quickly ousted from his position. Paradoxically, he achieves these practical results with seemingly impractical methods, for he seeks help not from some earthly source, but by trafficking in the unseen worlds. Our difficulties, so the shaman believes, come because we are out of harmony with the spirit realms. Everything on earth has its beginning and end in the world of the spirit; our time on earth is only a brief sojourn. The shaman's task is to help his tribe remember their roots and realize the profound wisdom and strength that is available through spiritual practices.

The art of shamanism is almost always accompanied by music of some sort: drumming, chanting, dancing, the playing of simple stringed instruments or woodwinds. It is not only in Africa that music and religious ritual are connected. Throughout the world, music has been revered for its healing powers, its ability to provoke trance states, and its power to bridge the gap between the sacred and the profane. Some anthropologists believe that ". . . music came into existence from the desire of primitive peoples to have a special language other than ordinary speech for communication with the supernatural."[4] From our earliest days, music has fulfilled spiritual functions; only recently have humans begun to view it as a purely aesthetic phenomenon.

> In Black Africa, any work of art is at the same time a magic operation. The aim is to enclose a vital force in a tangible casing and, at the appropriate moment, release this force by means of dance or prayer.
>
> —Leopold Senghor[5]

Whenever I observe people at a concert I am always struck by this truth: that what people are really looking for is some kind of magic, something to lift them out of their drab, ordinary world and into a realm of more intense feeling within themselves and deeper intimacy with others. When others simply see a bar crowded with people looking for a little relief and a good time, I often feel the possibility of something more extraordinary, an electrically amplified shamanic ritual. The form may have changed in the last few thousand years, but the form is the least important element. Music has served a ritual function for thousands of years, and just because most people have forgotten doesn't change that fact. Our ever-reliable bass player, Tina Zuccarello (formerly Capellini), experienced this power first hand at a gig a few years ago. In a personal interview she admitted:

> For a long time I'd known that music, and the blues especially, could heal people in some way. For me, it was a great theory until I really saw it happen big. The gig at the Peer R&B Festival in Belgium drew a whole different crowd from the jazz lovers of Nice, many of whom were rich and famous. Peer, on the other hand was a venue for a lot of people with nowhere else to go—hard-working blue-collar people, street people, even desperate people, the folks who know how hard it is to survive in this world; folks who aren't so protected from their pain.
>
> And there we were, in front of five or six thousand of them. They screamed, cheered, raised their beer glasses, moved to the beat we laid down. Maybe it was the sheer numbers that did it for me. All of a sudden the reality of their lives, their hopes and dreams, and the dead-ends they were constantly coming up against washed over me like a huge wave. It was almost unbearable until I realized that our music was making a difference for them—consoling something deep in their souls, helping them remember something essential they had forgotten long ago. They were touched, changed, happy for the space of a few

moments or a few hours. There was hope.

This is what keeps me coming back to the stage. I don't much care about being in the spotlight. I like it, but I don't need applause. But to know that I can help give life or even love to people and share life and love from them, well, it makes it possible for me to get up in the morning when we've been gigging until 3 A.M. and have to get back on the road at 7.

For me, the blues isn't about hearing. The blues is about feeling! I feel the music in the hollow place under my ribs—in my chest and around my heart. I feel the music in my gut. I can sense when the audience feels it too because all of a sudden we are together. Sound energy, that's what it is. It gets into the body and it changes things. I know something about vibrational healing—how sounds can affect the cells, the immune system, the health of the various organs, the bones. I think we have no idea how much power music has. The blues beat is a real medicine.

Blues pianist Roosevelt Sykes spoke about this healing power in plain words:

> Blues is like a doctor. A blues player . . . plays for the worried people . . . Like the doctor works from the outside of the body to the inside of the body. But the blues works on the insides of the inside.[6]

The term "musical physicianer," common around the turn of the twentieth century, points to this belief that music can have healing powers.

Sound Magic

The use of music as a potentiator for healing goes way back. Shamans, who are usually the master musicians of the tribe, attest that their art was taught to them by beings from other worlds. They see music as a gift from the gods. Blues lore also records mysterious meetings with supernatural entities. Many of the early blues singers were convinced of the possibility of this exchange with "the devil," especially in the case of the young and amazingly talented Robert Johnson. After the tragic death of his young wife, he left town one day barely able to play the guitar. When he returned only two years later, he was so far beyond everyone else that they could only explain his gifts by supernatural help. It is also worth noting that the Gypsies believe their music is a magical force that originated with the devil, a being they call Beng. These infernal myths attest to the fact that music is not only a bridge to the spiritual, but that it is a bridge through the "underworld" elements of life. That is a very different path to the divine than the one most of us in Western culture have grown up with, which presupposes that getting to heaven means getting as far away from hell as we possibly can. But the terrain that the shaman travels (as well as the bluesman and the Gypsy musician) is fraught with paradox: he prefers to get to heaven *through* hell.

There are four uses of music within the context of shamanic ritual. The first is as an aid to shifting the shaman's awareness. To make contact with the spirit worlds, the shaman must enter into a trance state, losing consciousness of his ordinary persona which keeps him tied to this reality. He is an expert technician in this regard. Alcohol or other drugs are often used, but almost always the drone of a drum, constant shaking of a rattle, repetition of a chant or the whine of a bow across a string accompanies the shaman on his or her journeys. Curt Sachs says that in tribal ceremonies:

> ... the instruments stand for the mystic realms of
> the sun and the moon, for the all-creative male and
> female principles, for fertility, rain, and wind; and
> they act as the strongest charms at man's disposal
> when he performs the vital rites of magic to protect
> his health and existence.[7]

Often shamans refer to their drum or other primary instrument as a horse or eagle, signifying the crucial role it serves in carrying the shaman to special, otherwise unreachable places.

The second function of the music is for the audience. The music helps to focus the attention of the tribe and to align its members with the purpose of the shaman. The shaman and his musician-helpers create a mood through music, and the more people fall into it, the stronger the mood becomes. The shaman uses the energy of the group by drawing the diffused attention into one direct beam of power. Then he will have more available energy to ride his drum into the other worlds and gather the wisdom and healing that the tribe needs. And, of course, the more the audience is in sync with the state of mind of the shaman, the more open they will be to his communication.

The third function of the songs is as a repository of the collective wisdom of the tribe, and of the teachings the shaman has accumulated in his journeys. The songs are maps showing how to enter into the spirit worlds and gain power there, and they teach how to use this power skillfully in daily life. The songs tell of the creation of the world and of human beings, and they tell of the history of the tribe. They describe how one becomes a shaman, and give people a solid grasp of who they are and their purpose in life. For thousands of years before we wrote down our most profound religious thoughts and feelings, we sang them.

The fourth function of the shaman's song is as a literal cry to heaven (or hell). The shaman is knocking on the gates of the unseen worlds, and his song is his calling card: it announces his coming, states his purpose, asks for help and promises something in return. For the tribal community, as well as for the rocking black churches, this communion with the Unseen was literal and palpable. It was a message that was sent with one's whole body, and singing it out seemed most effective. As one old woman in a southern black church described it, "The body can be used as a trumpet for the spirit."[8]

Shamanism is religion stripped down to the bones, the essential elements. By identifying these elements we can understand more clearly what is going on in the rituals of more complex, "developed" cultures, where these principles still profoundly inform our acts with meaning and purpose. Rogan Taylor believes that the origins of performance arts such as music, theater and dance are all linked to shamanism.[9] As the art of shamanism died out in Europe, performing artists retained many of the functions of the tribal medicine men and women, for shamanism was always accompanied by music, dancing, magic feats—any kind of spectacle that could grip people's attention. Taylor theorizes that the stunning explosion of rock and roll in 1950s' America was less about music than we think, and more about a need for body-based spirituality, which was seeking a channel for expression and fulfillment. African American music *is* body-based spirituality, and once white Americans caught on, there was no stopping them.

Shaking Hands With the Devil

African shamans once walked this land. Actually, some African tribes purposefully sold shamans into slavery to get rid of them. Even in tribal cultures, the shaman's ways were not always welcome, for the shaman was always willing to throw out social convention for the sake of higher truths. Elders from the Dahome tribe reported to anthropologists: "You have nearly all the people of this family in your country. They knew too much magic. We sold them because they made too much trouble."[10]

But, uprooted from their deep roots in Africa and transplanted to a land that literally denied their existence, post-African shamans were severely handicapped. There were many impediments to the practice of the shaman's art: the loss of the oral tradition; the need to keep their knowledge and power a secret from the white overlords (who would surely destroy any slave they believed had power); the absence of traditional musical instruments, power objects and healing herbs. But the final stroke was that shamanism was subsumed by a worldview that made its practice nearly impossible, the Western worldview which denied the existence of spirits, of ecstatic ritual and trance states. Luckily, some elements of African shamanism have survived through music.

The American black community had an urgent need which called forth the shaman, the one who would literally recreate the rituals needed to bring a reconciliation of soul and spirit, individual and tribe, human and cosmos. This is where the blues came in. A musical form this highly developed, widespread and popular didn't just happen. It served a function for the community, filled a need, and the bluesmen and women were well aware of this need.

Communal ritual revolving around music had filled important life-sustaining functions in Africa for hundreds, even thousands of years. The forms that have appeared in America—jazz, blues, gospel, and now rap—are fulfilling a similar function. Out of all of these genres, blues has so far proven to be the most universal, the music that speaks to the common people everywhere. For the blacks who created the blues, their music served as a vehicle to journey into an underworld of unimaginable torment, with the hope of release from their suffering—a kind of salvation of the streets. Maybe that's why they call it "the devil's music," because it takes us down into our own hell. In the shamanic worldview though, getting to know "the devil" may be useful or even necessary for one's spiritual progress.

> I'm going down yonder
> behind the sun
> Gonna do some things there
> Ain't never been done
>
> Hold back the lightnin'
> With the palm of my hand
> Shake hands with the devil
> Make him crawl in the sand.
> —Koko Taylor, *I'm a Woman*[11]

This lyric from Koko Taylor, high priestess of Chicago blues, still belies the attitude that the devil is a bad guy, but it also describes a journey into the netherworlds that would seem sinful by Christian standards. "Shaking hands with the devil" is what the blues is about: making friends with our nastiness, gaining the power necessary to deal with our darkest emotions. This kind of activity was not fully accepted at the local church. But for Koko, befriending the devil and then making him crawl in the sand seems to be a prerequisite for her to be able to shout: I'm a Woman. Her lyrics read like some ancient shamanic scripture.

The blues is America's road to hell, a place we are mightily afraid to go. In the shamanic traditions, it is a given that our soul needs not only the clear light of the heavens, but also the dark, passionate forces of Hades. Like Christianity, and almost all religions, shamanism has a concept of heaven and hell. But unlike Western religions, shamanism imposes no moral dichotomy. Hell, or the underworld, is a dark, fertile, chaotic place, full of vitality and creativity. It is the source of the earth's fecundity, man's drive to create, woman's sexual power. In shamanism, hell, not heaven, is the place of transformation, the place to get our ticket for a new life. But the price is high. One has to endure all one's inner demons and make friends with them, because it is they, ironically, who hold the keys for transformation.

In my travels with Shri, I have had plenty of opportunities to make friends with my demons—we've played some pretty low-down places. Time after time, I have been amazed at the fearlessness and natural openness that the women in the band carry into these threatening circumstances. Of course, sometimes forceful measures need to be taken, like the time Tina had to jab some "slimeball" (to use her exact terminology) in the stomach with the neck of her bass, to keep him from "sliming" (her word again) all over her. Or the time some drunk crawled up onstage, and Deborah, still singing into the microphone, started walking straight toward him with a menacing look in her eyes. In his hasty retreat, I think I witnessed the first-ever stage dive at a blues show.

But generally, we have been able to turn potentially troublesome situations like these to our advantage, not by fighting but by embracing them, like the time when a bachelor party threatened to drown out the music with its loud, drunken revelers. One sorely inebriated man was definitely looking for trouble, and I could tell it was only a matter of time before he pissed someone off and provoked a fight. Amid all the hooting and hollering, Deborah threw out a hook over the mike: "Hey, you guys look like you need some women."

"Say what?" retorted the head partyer. "This is a bachelor party," he enunciated carefully.

"A basketball party?" she replied innocently, not missing a trick.

"No! No! Bachelor! Bachelor Party!"

"Oh."

After talking with the drunk for a little while, Deborah agreed to let him come up on break and do a rap number. Now she had this guy eating out of the palm of her hand. As Deborah began singing again, he actually got down on his hands and knees and crawled across the dance floor toward her as if she was his only hope. When he got just a few feet from the stage he just stayed there (to her relief), reclining on the floor with his head propped up with his hand, gazing up lovingly. What a turn around! Deborah had reclaimed the space not by barking orders, but by sheer magnetism.

There have been several times like this when situations could have gotten ugly, only to be saved by friendly gestures on our part. I remember one guy, so drunk he could barely stand, who came within inches of us while we played. He yelled unintelligible (and probably unmentionable) things, tried to get the women in the band to dance with him, assaulting us with his alcohol-laden breath. Usually, I am completely repelled by guys like this, but this time I did something out of character. During one of my solos, I walked out and played just for him. As I wailed away on my guitar he leaned one arm on my shoulder, tottering dangerously as he closed his eyes and reveled in the music. I could feel the heat of his painful alcohol haze rising out of him, and each note that I played seemed to feed his hungry heart. After a minute or so, he opened his eyes, sauntered over to the bar and sat down, never to bother us again. "Why didn't I ever get it before?" I thought to myself. These guys are the kinds of people the blues really speaks to: they don't want to hurt anyone, they just want a little relationship, a little recognition of who they are in a world that is threatening to blot out their very existence. We all need a little magic in our lives.

Land of the Hoodoo Men

Now, Chile, if you go wanderin' the blue bayous
You'd better take a mojo offering with you.

—Hoodoo Slim

Belief in magical powers garnered through deals with the devil, or other shady activity, was still common in the early 1900s, and was referred to as *hoodoo*, certainly a variation on the word "voodoo," which itself derives from the African American religion Voudun. Several African religions have migrated across the ocean and merged with elements of Christianity and Native American religion, especially in Latin America: Haitian Voudun and Brazilian Santeria are two of these religions which are still vital and thriving today. Africans in Latin America could continue practicing their native religions because, in Catholicism, the veneration of the saints with its profusion of rituals and idols created a perfect camouflage for the African *loas* (gods), allowing the Africans to actually worship the *loas* by equating them with Catholic saints, right under the noses of the priests. Most importantly, Catholics did not ban drumming, which was absolutely essential for religious ritual. It is said that "... the religious music of the African American cults is often *indistinguishable* from the music of the parent faiths in West Africa."[12]

On the American continent, however, native African religions all but died out. The stark ritual of Protestantism provided scant cover for any would-be shamans. The one place where Voudun continued to thrive was the only predominantly Catholic city in the country: New Orleans. This city certainly was an anomaly; it also was home to the largest number of free blacks in the South. It is no accident that the Voudun capital of the American continent is also the birthplace of jazz, the most highly original music this country has produced.

A word needs to be spoken about jazz, because like the blues, it too has served a spiritual function for its players and listeners alike. Jazz exists because one day a bunch of black guys commandeered a European ensemble tradition, threw out the sheet music, and replaced it with gut feeling as the driving force behind the music. The rules of music meant nothing to them compared to the urgency and hunger that moves musicians to heights of pure excess and reckless enthusiasm. Esoteric scales and fancy techniques aren't the point of jazz; they've certainly been employed, but the sensitive jazz player uses them only as means to an end, never for their own sake.

Blues and jazz play with the notes and the rhythmic structure because they are more concerned with emulating the infinite variegations of human emotion than with some arbitrary musical system. If the music that remains within the staff lines is meant to soothe the savage beast, then non-Western music's task is to unleash it. If anything is truly savage about this beast, it is a savage joy, a wild passion for life that obliterates all Western sensibilities, social *and* musical. We can parrot the most wise and profound philosophy on the planet, but if there's no feeling behind it we might as well be reading the phone book. As Charlie Parker once said, "If you haven't lived it, it won't come out of your horn." The best jazz always has one foot in the mud of the blues, with its roots in field hollers, rockin' spirituals and African ritual music.

I've heard John Coltrane pieces in which, if I close my eyes, it sounds like a bunch of infernal demons wrestling with each other in the pits of hell, pushing against each others' sound until it feels as if the whole song could break wide open and swallow me whole. Or, as if a storm had descended in the middle of the stage and the band was gathered around it trying to contain it, exorcise it, use its energy, ride the storm to previously unknown heights of expression. Coltrane's music has an energy that could turn on him at the least slip of his mastery. And I'm not only talking about his mastery as a musician; here we enter the realm of the conjure men, tamers of elemental forces normally beyond our control. For visionaries like Coltrane, music is more than music; it is their shamanic tool for calling down and handling this wild energy.

Not only jazz players exuded this aura of hoodoo charm and power. Blues players too have commonly been associated with dark magical gifts. It is no accident that the birthplace of the blues, the Mississippi Delta, is located only a few hundred miles up the Mississippi River from New Orleans. At the beginning of the 1900s, the area between Memphis and New Orleans (the birthplaces of rock and roll and jazz, respectively) was teeming with both hoodoo practitioners and musical pioneers. Almost all the blues (and blues-inspired) legends that we know of today were born in or near this area: Muddy Waters, BB King, Albert King, Bo Diddley, Elvis Presley, Howlin' Wolf, Robert Johnson, Son House, Charlie Patton, Willie Dixon, Otis Rush, Magic Sam, Charlie Musselwhite, Sonny Boy Williamson—the list is staggering.

New Orleans and the Delta had the highest incidence of African-isms in the country, cultural patterns that survived virtually intact from Africa. One of these is a makeshift instrument called the diddley bow (Could this be where Bo Diddley gets his name?). It consists simply of a metal string tied between two nails, usually assembled directly onto the wall or floor of a house. The house itself acts as the resonator of the sound, and a bottle sliding along the string produces the notes. Countless blues guitarists have identified the diddley bow as the first instrument they ever played. One-stringed fiddles and lutes (called *bentwas*) are common all over Africa, but, curiously, the only place in America this instrument is found is in Mississippi. This was due to its isolation combined with the strong African music of nearby New Orleans. The spirit of Africa was strong in Mississippi—that spirit that combined magic and music, sex and holiness into a frighteningly powerful force.

In fact, even today Mississippi is producing bluesmen and women who still shine with this primordial radiance. R.L. Burnside is one such Mississippi native. His songs are simple, direct and hard-edged, with an insistent, driving pulse that can't be stopped. A disciple of the roll and tumble spirituals of Fred McDowell, R.L., going strong in his seventies, is taking blues in a whole new direction. He recently recorded an album with the Jon Spencer Blues Explosion, a punk/blues band with the swagger of an early Elvis. R.L. has reached a point where his music is absolutely unique: unequivocally steeped in the Mississippi/African tradition of highly-charged, polyrhythmic one-chord romps, it also captures the freshness, simplicity and drive of early rock and roll (some songs you would swear were straight punk, fast and furious). Maybe that would explain the scores of young people at his gigs who normally wouldn't be found anywhere near a blues club. Amazingly, R.L.'s songs have barely changed from when he first recorded them thirty years ago. He just switched from acoustic to electric guitar, kicked up the volume and the tempo, and suddenly his music sounds like some kind of proto-rock and roll, an original link between the blues and modern music (or possibly what rock might have sounded like in a parallel universe, if different events had transpired).

From the moment he barks out the first notes on his mojo guitar we're catapulted into another world—R.L.'s domain of ancient boogie, terminal trance, psychotic alcohol haze and bad jokes. "Well, well, well!" he ritually intones between each song. He says they call him "Mr. Wizard" because he puts a spell on you. His music is *all* beat. There is no escape—you *will* surrender to the god of rhythm! Like other Mississippi natives, whose music is tinged with the mood of gospel and soul, R.L.'s music is steeped in the spiritual life of the deep South, in his case, conjuring images of the mysterious bayous and their hoodoo men. With blues artists like him around, I'm not worried about the impending death of the blues; in fact, I'm sure the blues will keep on telling its story until the end of time.

R.L. plays regularly at a local juke joint (formerly a Sanctified church) owned by fellow bluesman Junior Kimbrough, whose music has been called "disturbing" and out of tune. Charlie Feathers, who wrote songs for Elvis Presley and was deeply influenced by Kimbrough in his youth, has called him "the beginning and end of music." Kimbrough describes his own style like this:

> My songs they have just one chord, there's none
> of that fancy stuff you hear now, with lots of chords
> in one song. If I find another chord I leave it for
> another song. My songs don't come from the music I
> hear outside. It comes from inside myself.[13]

Kimbrough's sound must be heard to be believed. His musical heritage goes back further than thought can reach, to the primal rhythms of the heartbeat, the rumble of antelope bounding across the plain, the crackle of thunder—he is the sound of nature itself.

Half a century ago, when R.L. started playing, he recalls that ". . . 'round here was mostly drum music, there wasn't many people playing the guitar at all."[14] R.L. grew up in one of the richest veins of African culture this country has ever seen. He and the other musicians from his region—Junior Kimbrough, Jesse Mae Hemphill, Fred McDowell—all have a ferocious, hypnotic intensity that is unique even to the rest of Mississippi. Jesse Mae Hemphill's grandfather, Sid Hemphill, was famous all around the area for his fife and drum music, some of the most peculiar music ever heard on this continent. Jesse Mae says that her ". . . grandaddy's music, it come from Africa.

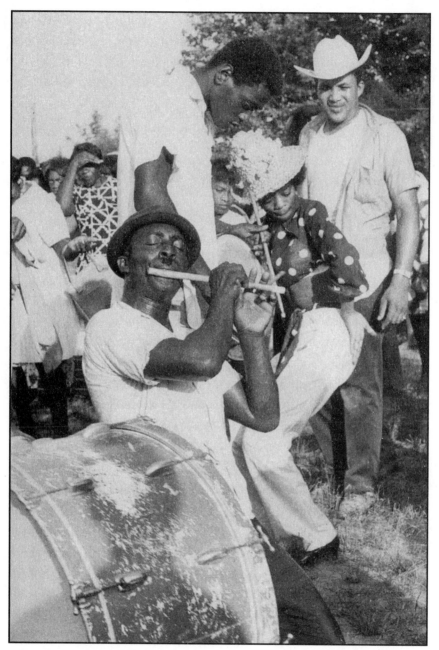

Napoleon Strickland, one of the few torch bearers of the fife and drum tradition.

My grandaddy knowed it, and his daddy knowed it too. Grandaddy use to play his drums everywhere . . ."[15] Sid's father, Doc Hemphill, grew up in New Orleans and resettled in northern Mississippi, transplanting a vibrant voodoo drum tradition into this fertile, isolated hill country. Over a century later, it is still having strong repercussions on American music.

Johnny Shines, Robert Johnson's best friend and musical accompanist, spoke of his awe of Howlin' Wolf and the near supernatural aura he projected:

> I didn't know it at the time, but Wolf was a tractor driver. As far as I knew, he could have crawled out of a cave . . . I thought he was a magic man, he looked different than anyone I'd seen, and I come along and say a guy that played like Wolf, he sold his soul to the devil.[16]

Robert Johnson (and others) claimed to have met the devil at a lonely crossroads at midnight to gain their musical prowess, and their stories seem to have been taken at face value by the people who knew them best. This story has its roots in ancient African Voudun worship, where the crossroads refers to the intersection point between the spiritual and earthly realms. Before one can invoke the spirits into one's body, one must pay a toll to the keeper of the crossroads, Legba, the most important god in all invocational ceremonies, for without his cooperation the door between the worlds will remain closed and nothing will happen. Legba is a trickster god in Yoruba myth, always getting us humans into trouble. In the Americas:

> Legba became identified with the Devil of Christianity early on. Slave lore often depicted the

Devil as a trickster figure, more like Legba with his mordant sense of humor and his delight in chaos and confusion than the more somber and threatening Devil portrayed in hellfire-and-brimstone sermons.

—Robert Palmer[17]

Johnson's verses testify that he was plagued by spiritual conflict, and that he sincerely believed he had a relationship with the devil. It is within the realm of possibility that what Johnson was talking about wasn't literally a deal with the devil, but an apprenticeship to Legba and the practices of Voudun, which, after all, were equated with the devil's ways by the Christian community. What was he doing those two years between the time he could hardly play a lick and the night he returned, acknowledged guitar wizard, bluesman? Was he wandering the blue bayous with a mojo offering in his hand? We will never know. But we do know that those who had an intense spiritual need *and* a calling to play the blues were shut out of the black church; they were forced to work out their spiritual salvation through other means, the ways of the mysterious hoodoo men.

Early blues songs, like this one by Hoodoo Slim, are filled with reference to the arcana of hoodoo practice: mojos, goofer dust, charms and curses.

I been long gone
on Hoodoo charms and spells
I get a thrill
When the devil rings my bell
Gypsy women do with me what they will
'Cause I found and broke the Seventh Seal

—Hoodoo Slim

And in these next lines, Salome Arnold takes the Voodoo blues to new depths:

> I had this Gypsy boy, you see
> He was always touchin' me
> He warmed my body, cooled my mind
> He had me thinkin' that I was Divine
>
> He had me drinkin' Urban Voodoo Juice
> I tried to get to California but he wouldn't cut me
>   loose
> He took my mind apart and put it back together
>   again
> My baby's got me hooked on that ole Urban
>   Voodoo Juice again!

Sounds like these people really knew how to get into trouble! These verses witness to the existence of an occult world none of us ever read about in history books, a world of magical practices that our ancestors thought they had exterminated from this continent along with the Native Americans. What could Hoodoo Slim be referring to when he says he "found and broke the Seventh Seal"? And what about Salome Arnold's line, "He took my mind apart and put it back together again." I don't think these people were simply playing around with love potions and good luck amulets. They're talking about revelatory knowledge here, real power. There was real Voudun being practiced on this continent, and these lines testify that there were some blues singers who, cast out of their community churches, were at least familiar with these practices.*

*For a more recent example of the use of voodoo imagery in black music, take another listen to Bo Diddley's *Who Do You Love?* With all his talk about "rat-

Cry of the Soul

A shaman might be described as someone who has an inner *daimon*, or muse, whose communication is so all-encompassing that it cannot fit into any of the conventional channels. Some of those who have vacillated between preaching and playing the blues or rock and roll are good examples. They want to speak all aspects of the human being: our spiritual heights, swampy depths, sexual passions and the ordinariness of everyday life. Many of these visionaries cannot live up to the immense demands of their calling. They may crack under pressure, become eccentrics. It takes someone with crystal clear vision to hold this kind of immense inner tension and channel it into a new form that encompasses both the sacred and the profane. Only then can it accomplish the shaman's task, which is to help restore a feeling of wholeness to those who have lost their way.

Music, for some mysterious reason, happens to be a great vehicle for this kind of healing communication, and the most beloved performers are those who can use their art to deliver this message, to bring people to all the places they need to go inside themselves. Blues music is especially suited for this task of embracing all aspects of life because it is rooted in the earth, both the soil of the South steeped in lives of hardship, and the dark loam of Africa, rich with the history of a proud and dignified race. There is so much in the blues that is left unsaid—primeval emotions, eternal dramas—as if the whole history of humankind could be poured into one song. And when that song is sung by one who has lived the story, the singer brims over with long-forgotten strains of anguish, shared dreams and broken promises. Some of those compositions are universal: their story reaches far from the time and place of their inception, as if their roots had been slowly snaking their way through the collective soul

tlesnake hides," "tombstones," and "human skulls," it is obvious that the title song is really a play on *Hoodoo Your Love*.

for a million years to finally emerge one day into pure song.

We love music because it sings the longing within ourselves that we have buried under so much distraction. It is transcendent *within* the body, not transcendent *of* the body. Powerful, heartfelt music can lead us back through years of encrusted cynicism and despair to a pristine innocence. Many of us have worked long and hard to wall off that innocence so that we can protect ourselves from feeling the pain of having it stomped on by senseless ignorance and brutality. Music, especially the blues, contains a distant echo of that first innocence as it sings its way through the heartbreaks and emotional detritus of modern life. The blues is not only sincere, but it has the power to change us, for real, and for the better. As Freud learned one hundred years ago, we can learn a lot by listening to each others' stories. And real art, real music, real blues, is so full of the crazy grace of humanity that we have to listen.

Unless it has been wounded beyond repair, the soul will not lie dormant. Every night in our dreams it bubbles up images to alert us to a vibrant, sensual world inside us. Dreams are the language of the soul and they're trying to get our attention. As insistent as our nightly dream life, our incessant music-making as a species is also a cry of the soul. Music speaks the soul's language and that is why we are so attracted. Today it is everywhere (albeit in mostly disembodied electronic forms). It calms our nerves in elevators, announces the brand new luxury car on television, chimes when we turn on our computer, makes our morning commute smoother and provides the mood for a romantic dinner. Because we are surrounded by it, we take it for granted. We have lost touch with "the soul thang," the real reason for its existence. We have a bite of the meal when we could have the whole feast. A little soul keeps us sane, but too big a dose can be scary because when we enter the soul's domain, we give up our comfort and control.

S h r i ' s   H o o d o o   M a n

Back in July '97 we played a blues festival in another small French
town, Montmorillon. After a sumptuous French picnic of roasted
chicken and fresh vegetables (followed by some authentic French ice
cream, of course), we started playing to a packed room. The local
turnout was quite good—a blues band from the States is a pretty big
event in some of these small towns.

The club had the ambiance of an old-time jazz lounge, a dark,
almost gloomy room crammed with antique tables and chairs. From
the stage, all I could see were vague outlines of expectant faces gathered around the flickering candlelight which adorned each table. The
haze of cigarette smoke, combined with the moody blue and red
spotlights, added to the sensuous and mysterious atmosphere. We
were very excited to play, especially since Lee, our wildcard, would be
joining us on two songs.

We kicked into a strong, energetic set. Lee snuck up on stage
early, taking hold of Deborah's tambourine and shaking it up at the
back of the stage, invisibly juicing the space. By the time his first song
came up—a duet with Deborah called *Off Limits*, full of plucky ban-
ter and sexual innuendo, we were all feeling pretty hot in that little
room. *Off Limits* is about a man trying to get what he wants, and the
woman telling him how she wants him to be before he can get it—
the eternal drama.

Lee: Hey now mama
what you mean it's off limits
hold on sugar
listen to me one minute
ain't we lovers
should have nothin' to hide
I know you ain't frozen

and for sure you ain't shy

Deborah: Listen here daddy
these is modern times
you wanna be a caveman
you can forget what is mine
got to take it easy
got to take it just right
no rollin' over sleepin'
before it's even midnight

Lee has fun with this song. He makes up verses on the spot, inciting Deborah to get as outrageous as he does. Even with the language barrier the crowd is all grins; Lee's and Deborah's body language and playful mood together lets them know exactly what is going on. Then Lee turns around to me—it's solo time! I don't come in on full strength, and he quickly lets me know that's not good enough. He stretches his arms toward me, his hands beckoning toward himself, saying "Come on, Ed," seducing me, demanding. Suddenly, he is the woman in the song saying, "No rollin' over sleepin' before it's even midnight." In this moment, I cannot resist. It feels like he's pulling my real self out from behind these artificial walls I've built up to keep my expression within "acceptable" limits. I've got to "Use it or lose it." A string comes flying off my guitar as I push my glass slide beyond the notes, past the threshold of speech.

Next comes the song *Little Red Rooster*, written by Willie Dixon. Lee has truly made this song his own. He barks and moans the words with complete conviction, exhorting everyone to help him find his lost rooster, "too lazy for days." The intense underworld quality of his sexual urgency destroys all our romantic notions of love—I half expected all the women to start running for their lives. Actually, women seem to appreciate this quality of Lee's, his ability to completely expose what men really want and get beyond all the bullshit mating games. I love when he lets it loose too, because he brings so much humor and total lack of shame to an issue that gets men into a lot of trouble.

I flashed on another gig months before in our Arizona hometown. Lee was singing this same song, and as one reporter described his rendition that night, ". . . his growls erupted inside like liquid raw heat at the center of the body." An older black woman named Ging, who had spent many years in the music business was at that performance (in the forties she was the lead singer for a band that opened for the InkSpots), and as soon as Lee started singing she sat bolt upright, riveted to the swaying of his body and his fiercely erotic play. As the same reporter noted: "After the song was over, Ging turned to me, the corners of her mouth curled upward in a huge smile, her face looking radiant. Referring to Lee, she said, 'That was the hoochie koochie man!'" Walking over to him after the gig, Ging "looked right at him and said, 'Oooohwee, you woke me up!'" Seems like that has always been the shaman's job.

Back in Montmorillon it is time for me to do another solo, and Lee is again right there, completely in my face, egging me on. I've already broken one string, but I can still do a lot with the two treble strings I have left, letting the slide wail and moan the pain, rage and sexual energy I've repressed all my life. Lee is beckoning me again— he wants it back!

Another string breaks. "Now I'm really screwed!" I think to myself. As I choke out the last few desperate notes of the solo, Lee deftly takes one of the broken strings hanging from the neck of my guitar, brings his head in close, and wraps the string around his neck, pretending to pull it tight while he makes ridiculous choking faces! (And all this without the slightest tugging on my guitar.) I am immediately thrown into a struggle of keeping it together while Lee is pantomiming hanging himself right in front of me and the whole audience. (Amazingly, few people I talked to afterwards noticed Lee doing this at all!) My initial shock was quickly followed by fear, total disbelief, and lastly complete confusion. First he wants me to make him bleed, and now this. Fear is gripping me, too dramatic and intense to let go of. I feel like I'm swimming in deep waters, far from shore. My mind is simply trying to gain a foothold on reality by trying to make sense of it all, while another part of me tries to just accept it in all its shocking glory.

Lee somehow seems to know just how to throw me off balance, stopping my comfortable habitual patterns dead in their tracks, opening me up to new ways of seeing things. His outrageous ways do the same for other band members, and with our audiences too. Being led into the dense jungle of our primal feelings can be another kind of healing, where we see parts of ourselves that we have been avoiding—the pain and fear that have been running our lives unbenownst to our conscious awareness. We have to be ready for anything, even the unknown. The blues is just a springboard from which to jump into life. When we jump, we never know what we'll find: one night ecstasy, the next night hell, maybe a string of nights where nothing seems to happen at all. But it doesn't matter so much *what* happens as long as we are there, clear-eyed and present for the show of life.

I see now that my attraction to music is that somehow (and to say that I know precisely *how* would just be empty theory) it allows me to feel safe enough to let this primal terror and grief well up, to accept my brokenness. The words of that Elmore James song still haunt me: "Do you know what it's like to be alone . . ."

Some nights the blues is about hanging out in the tavern of hopelessness, waiting.

Chapter 5

Music of Longing Around the World

*Flamenco is the means through which man reaches
God without the intervention of saints or angels.*
—Luis Antonio de Vega[1]

The story has been repeated many times. The poor and disenfranchised sing about their troubles, creating raw, sensual, passionate music. The songs are a part of who they are, inseparable from the entire cultural weave from which they arise: the fields, the streets, the dialect, the dance styles and mating games. The songs provide strength and sustenance because they bring people together to share their common feelings. Singing their "blues" brings not only comfort and release but solidarity as well.

Then the unexpected happens. The music's popularity grows beyond caste boundaries, capturing the hearts of the nation, making other music seem stale in comparison. Soon, it is being lauded as a "national" music. Meanwhile, the people who created it are no better off, except for a few lucky musicians who find success. Highly polished and refined versions of this music hit the airwaves all over the world, while the same peasants and workers, unfazed, continue singing whatever they feel like with their five-dollar guitars.

America is not the only place that has blues music: many countries around the world have given birth to their own brand of soul-soothing music that rises deep from the earth and carries one's heart on the wind. In Portugal, the blues they sing is called *fado*; in Greece, it is *rebetica*; and the tango, which sings of the sufferings of love, is unquestionably the blues of Argentina. Here the tragic/ecstatic play of love between man and woman is also portrayed in taut, sensual, stylized dance. In every case, the "blues" begins in the taverns and whorehouses, the mean streets of the city, and slowly filters its way into the rest of the country. In the case of the tango, the Argentine middle class scorned it because of its disreputable roots. Only when the music made it to Paris and garnered international acclaim did it find greater acceptance at home.

The blues has had a similar journey. In the sixties, blues artists whose star had been declining in their own country found Europe welcoming them with open arms. Soon, there was a blues "revival" among young white groups in England. The Beatles, The Rolling Stones and many other seminal British rock groups lived off a steady diet of blues, R & B and soul. But when these groups got to the U.S.A. they were shocked that our own blues greats were living in obscurity. Today, finally, after decades of neglect, the blues and jazz are being touted as our most original "American" music. Painful irony.

Gypsy Blues

If the blues has a first cousin, it would have to be the stirring music of the Gypsies of southern Spain. The parallels between the flamenco music of the Gypsies in Andalusia and the deep blues of African

Americans are striking, especially in the startling juxtaposition of moods that each genre conveys.

"[Flamenco]. . . bursts forth from these two mainspring feelings: fear of death and desire for love."[2] Blues can be described exactly the same way. As those notorious blue notes weave their melancholic melody of lament, a fierce, sexual backbeat builds up the erotic tension. We don't know whether to weep, dance or screw. The same kind of immense emotional tension permeates the cry of the Gypsies, for they share with the African Americans a strange fate—to have been deprived of their homeland (in the Gypsies' case, India). Living in a strange land, never really feeling at peace or accepted by the dominant culture, never feeling fully rooted in the earth, the Gypsies relied heavily on their music to keep their community together and to keep their souls alive and burning with passion. They have a saying that goes: "Stay wherever people sing, for evil folk have no song."

The Gypsies, who left India as early as the fifth century C.E., have always had a reputation as consummate musicians. Everywhere they went they inevitably affected the musical sensibilities of the region. Gypsies first spent a considerable amount of time in Iran where they ". . . contributed to the diffusion of Oriental musical instruments and styles towards both the Arabic world and the West."[3] In their wanderings they introduced the Arabic lute to Europe and brought in the clarinet from Turkey around 1820.

The Gypsy diaspora ranges from the Middle East and Northern Africa through most of Europe, as far north as Ireland. It is said that French Gypsies ended up in New Orleans (of all places!) in the early seventeenth century, and they are now scattered all over America as well. Every country has a different name for them—Les Tsiganes or Les Manouches in France, Los Gitanos in Spain, the Zingari in Italy, or, as some Gypsies call themselves, the Rom.

The Rom have an absolutely voracious musical appetite.

Wherever they go they master the local musical styles and alter them to fit their own melodic, rhythmic and cultural sensibilities. These adaptations then often find their way back into the "dominant" musical culture, the most notable example being the flamenco music of Spain. This pattern played itself out in America with the meeting of African and European cultures. African Americans adapted European music to suit their own ears, with no intention of transforming the entire American musical landscape; but that is exactly what happened. Alan Lomax said of the Gypsy songs that although they

> ... have their roots in Moorish music ... in their own setting, they are as much songs of protest as the blues of the American Negro. Like the blues, they are derived from work songs, and like them, too, they have come to dominate the popular music of the entire country.[4]

Another trait the Rom share with the African American culture (and many others) is that the lines between sacred and secular music become blurred. For instance, in Greece, the Rom

> ... did not only play hymns or patron saint's days; they played at weddings, christenings, and in the taverns at night. They went from house to house playing Christmas carols and Easter hymns. They were the only musicians present at every festival, every celebration. They brought life, joy and happiness to everyone taking part.
>
> — Nick Dawanellos[5]

Maybe the Gypsies also imported from the Middle East an Islamic sentiment about the dual and complementary uses of music: "Now for God and the Prophet, now for festivity and dancing."[6] In these cultures, a musician's training is incomplete if he or she cannot play for solemn religious occasions as well as wild, bacchanalian festivities.

Gypsies arrived in Spain in the early fifteenth century, at the tail end of an almost eight-hundred-year Islamic presence in that region. We can imagine the local reaction when a tribe of dark-skinned Gypsies would first arrive in a town with their shabby carts and animals, the women dressed in colorful, almost oriental garb, the men unkempt and wild, yet carrying a timeless dignity. Their almond-shaped eyes seemed to veil a secret, exotic world of magic and mysticism, and they would frequently capitalize on their mystique in order to swindle the *gadjos* (literally, bumpkins or farmers). In their all night bouts of singing and drinking it ". . . was not unusual for the enraptured Gypsies to tear their clothes and smash anything they got their hands on, driven as they were to a kind of collective madness."[7] People would either fear them or be fascinated, and the people who were attracted would make the others even more scared. Soon Gypsies were being hunted down and persecuted by the same authorities who perpetrated the Inquisition.

Curiously, as the laws against the Gypsies grew harsher, the affection of the common people increased in proportion. This same mixture of fear and envy, repulsion and attraction, has been directed at the bluesman from his earliest days, and also accompanied the beginnings of rock and roll. We see this attitude directed toward folk musicians everywhere, including the African *griots*, the tango dancers, and the wandering Indian bards: genuine sympathy for their free-spirited music simultaneous with scorn for their wayward, low-class lifestyle.

It is curious how universal this attitude of fear and envy is; similar to how the crazy-wise ways of the shaman are seen in tribal cultures—as a necessary evil. People run to the shaman when they need him, but they consider him a threat when everything is going smoothly, because the shaman lives according to higher laws than those of society, and he or she will break taboos when the situation calls for it. Similarly, the Gypsies have always been violently opposed to limitation of their freedom, for they know that to submit to a soulless bureaucracy is to lose their tenuous hold on ancient, sacred cultural patterns. Their music is one of the primary ways that they keep these spiritual principles alive, just as the blues and spirituals kept alive the souls of black Americans.

Gypsy songs convey the tragic sense of life, but also are filled with the power and conviction of soul survivors. The following lines sum up the function of their music as well as any:

> I sing not for attention,
> Nor because I have a good voice.
> I sing to prevent the fusing
> Of bitterness and sorrow.[8]
> —Gypsy lyric

In the U.S. and other Western cultures we habitually think of music as serving one of two aims: art or entertainment. In either case, the primary purpose is to please the listener by delivering a beautiful product. This is not so for other cultures. For the Gypsies, as well as for the Indians and the Africans, music must tell the truth. It must accurately reflect life, which is not always pretty.

> When we listen to . . . music we decide in our
> minds whether it is beautiful or ugly, but the Oriental
> asks himself whether it is a good or evil influence. He

does not consider the music from an aesthetic, but from a magical point of view, for the sound must enchant the audience.

— Walter Starkie, *Don Gypsy: Adventures with a Fiddle in Southern Spain* [9]

The Gypsy performer does not simply want to please the listener; he wants to work magic on him, to raise him out of his petty daily concerns and bring him to a place inside himself where feeling reaches a white hot intensity. Here is where human beings truly know themselves. In African American music this quality is called "soul." In flamenco, the word is *duende*, a mysterious and indefinable force that literally overtakes the best flamenco performers and radiates outward, infecting the audience as well. *Duende* produces

> . . . outrageous expressivity, a sound too human to be heard without a total upheaval of one's being, a heartrending cry that rips through the guts and transposes the listener to . . . sacred ecstasy. . . In the argot of flamenco, one does not say that a voice is beautiful, but rather that it "hurts"; it is not meant to please the listener, but to wound him like a dagger brandished in passion. [10]

Here, artistic creation is not a glorious act of inspiration from the heavenly Muse above. As the great Spanish poet Frederico Garcia Lorca put it:

> Angel and Muse approach from without; the Angel sheds light and the Muse gives form . . . but the Duende . . . must come to life in the nethermost

recesses of the blood. The Duende . . . will not approach at all if he does not see the possibility of death.[11]

So flamenco is not about being transported upward into realms of light and inspiration; it is an annihilating darkness. Only by totally abandoning oneself to the dark mystery of *duende* can the performance touch something in people that is completely real. The songs of the Gypsies touch the broken heart common to all humanity.

> I'm shedding more tears
> Than the river has water
> Because of almond black eyes
> That are my ruin
>   –Antonio Villodre[12]

Dancing the Blues

I first became aware of the connection between flamenco and the blues in 1997 when Shri was in southern France, just a few miles from the Spanish border. We were playing a theater that used to be a porno house—the walls were still painted dark red. The owner was from Russia—he spoke eight languages, owned most of the street (which was the main place of commerce in this small town), and he ran a Zen monastery up on the hill, in the midst of an ancient walled town. An interesting character. As we sat with him in the café (that he also owned) next to the theater, every imaginable type of music from around the world was playing on his CD player. That was when he mentioned that our music reminded him of flamenco. Not knowing too much about flamenco at the time, I wasn't sure what he was talking about. Shortly after this exchange I was lucky enough to see a performance, and I was blown away.

In the first couple of songs, the guitarists and drummers were just warming and nothing much was being stirred up. I was preparing myself for disappointment when a woman appeared in a long, colorful dress. She was proud, strong, yet not hiding her woundedness either. Her feet stamped the stage with thunderous force, almost as if saying to the earth, "I am here! I'm sending down roots. Support me, protect me." I was instantly reminded of the tremendous rootedness of The New Orleans Spiritualettes whom I had seen earlier that year. I felt that this Gypsy woman's dance was an expression of who woman is essentially. Her dancing came from her most intimate parts, from the pain of a lifetime, yet she did not wallow in her personal story. It seemed to me that she used her personal pain as a springboard to reach a more universal pain. As flamenco master Pedro Pena said, "You know how to express the song when you're carrying the pain of centuries with you. The Gypsy who knows how to do this gets it from his ancestors . . ."[13] A mountain of self-help books couldn't begin to tell me what she told me that night. I saw that in our best moments we disappear, and something bigger than us takes over.

That one dance would have been enough for me, but when she started singing I really got the connection to the blues. The minor key, the notes that slid and quavered, the dramatic pauses—it was all very bluesy. The mood was what really hit me: the cry of love that echoes into the endless night, the transformation of suffering into beauty and dignity, the singular will to live. I could easily see that the one rule of flamenco is "Don't hold anything back," that to go fully into the feeling was to leave the personal and enter into the universal. After being immersed in the blues for several years, hearing flamenco for the first time was like the joy of finding a long lost cousin. (I was reminded of the renowned French Gypsy guitarist Django

Reinhardt's reaction when he first heard the recordings of jazz trum-
peter Louis Armstrong: he took his head in his hands and wept, saying over and over *"Ach moune,"* literally "my brother.")

Some months after seeing this flamenco performance, I came
across a book by Samuel Charters about his travels in West Africa in
search of the roots of the blues. One passage drew such a concrete
parallel between flamenco and the blues that I quote it here at length:

> When I listened to Jali Nyama's performance . . .
> and to the songs of a halam player I'd recorded
> named Abdoulie Samba, I was surprised to hear how
> much Arabic influence there was in the music. The
> elaborate instrumental flourishes were all more
> Arabic than African. Some of the things I heard in it
> were also common to another Arab influenced style,
> the flamenco music of Spain. The kind of intensely
> brilliant instrumental passages that Jali Nyama played
> were like the guitar solos in a flamenco performance,
> and in Samba's playing there was display of virtuosi-
> ty using nearly every kind of technique that the fla-
> menco players used. When the blues first came to the
> notice of European intellectuals in the 1920's and
> 1930's there had been some comment about similar-
> ities between the blues and flamenco music . . . It was
> clear now that the West African musicians had already
> been influenced by Arabic music just as Gypsy singers
> and instrumentalists had been along the
> Mediterranean. The influence hadn't come from the
> Gypsies to the Mississippi blues men. There had been
> earlier Arabic music that had influenced them both
> . . .The songs I heard suggested that both the music

of today's griots . . . [the Spanish Gypsies] . . . and the bluesmen had the same common ancestry.[14]

I was stunned to learn that the amazing similarities among these three musical styles actually have historical roots. My passion for the blues was now taking me into unknown territory, because I was recognizing many of the same elements in folk music all over the world: all peoples spontaneously create music to soothe their suffering and give voice to their longing, for wherever we are on earth, when night falls we all see the same thing: an endless expanse of darkness filled with tiny points of light. The response is obvious: fill the heavens with the sound of beautiful, poignant voices. Call down the gods.

Bengali Blues

God has only one attribute. He's all Love.
—Sri Anirvan[15]

Only singing Baul songs doesn't make one a Baul.
—Pagol Ram Das, Baul[16]

If any one group of people have taken the human condition (otherwise known as the blues) to the heights of poetic and musical expression, it is the Bauls. They achieve this, I think, because their entire lives are about seeking the ultimate that the human heart has to offer. Rabindranath Tagore, India's most celebrated poet and Nobel laureate, "discovered" the Bauls in the early 1900s and brought them to world attention through his writings.

The Bauls are a small, eccentric group of wandering beggars, holy men and women, and musicians from Bengal, India. Their small notoriety is mainly due to their fiery devotional songs that captivate the hearts of the common people, as well as the hungry minds of folklore scholars. Their songs tell of the divine nature of human kind, and of their intense search for a love that does justice to our divinity within, what they refer to as the "Man of the Heart." Their attitude toward music is similar to that of the Sufis:

> Music is nothing less than the picture of the Beloved. It is because (of this) that we love music. But . . . what is our beloved? It is that which is our source and our goal.
>
> —Hazrat Inayat Khan[17]

The Bauls are generally comprised of lower caste people, "black sheep" we might say. These mad wanderers have dropped out of proper society and have chosen a life of the heart, dedicated to stoking the fires of spiritual passion within themselves and others. In some ways, they live an austere life, begging and playing music for their food; but at the same time, their spiritual path is an earthy, even lusty affair. Rather than decline worldly pleasure for the sake of spiritual gifts, they see human love as a mirror of and path to divine love. They hold that the energy of our sexuality comes from God, and it can take us back to God as well. Couples who have entered into the disciplines of this way practice seeing each other as reflections of the divine feminine or divine masculine. For the Bauls, God is found by accepting and celebrating the body, not by denying it.

Although there are no direct historical connections between the blues and the music of the Bauls, there are quite a few points of similarity:

1. the music is primarily about longing
2. the music comes from an outcast social group

3. it is nevertheless loved by the common people
4. lines drawn between the sacred and the carnal are blurred
5. the musicians who perform it are wanderers
6. the music is passionate and spontaneous
7. it addresses the intricacies of relationship between men and women

Significantly, the first time a Baul musician (Purna Das Baul) toured the U.S. was in 1969, as an intermission act for the Paul Butterfield Blues Band.

The Bauls of India: Invaders of the Heart

I search and search, alone I grieve
Meeting with many, but not with any.
Man of my Heart,
Where does he live?

—Sanatan Das Baul

These simple and vulnerable lines show the essence of Baul life as well as any: an unquenchable fire of longing suffuses their whole existence. Rather than try to forget or deny this tender pain, one who chooses the Baul way is called to dive deep into this well of grief within himself to find the elusive jewel that shuns the cold light of reason and the clammy palm of egoism. This treasure is the secret of all the longing and desire that a human being could experience, as if the yearning of an entire lifetime could be condensed into one tiny point of intense feeling, the light and heat of which is like an inner sun, burning up everything that comes near. This is the path of annihilation in love.

The Bauls uphold the love between Radha and Krishna as their
highest ideal. Krishna is none other than God himself, incarnated in
human form as a cowherd, and Radha is a *gopi*, a simple milkmaid
who is smitten with the young Krishna. The *Gita Govinda* (*Song of the
Cowherd*), written by the twelfth century mystic-poet Jayadeva,
describes their adolescent love dalliance in unparalleled, tender lyri-
cism. Yet, at the same time that this poetry broke through the boundaries of contemporary morality to deliver a love story of the highest
sensuality, it was also recognized as an inspired work of spiritual
metaphor. Jayadeva is now widely revered as a saint in India. In the
Gita Govinda, the common human emotions of infatuation, anguished
yearning and love are taken to their limits in order that one may use
these as a path to the Divine. The following passages give the reader
a taste of the Baul way.

First Radha reveals the total desperation of her love for Krishna:

> Sandalwood mountain wind,
> As you blow southern breezes
> To spread the bliss of love,
> Soothe me! End the paradox!
> Lifebreath of the world,
> If you bring me Madhava
> For a moment
> You may take my life!
> —*Gita Govinda* 7.39

Here, Krishna answers Radha's pleas and returns her love:

> Let pearls quivering on full breasts
> Move the depths of your heart!
> Let a girdle ringing on round hips

Proclaim the command of Love!
Radha, cherished love,
Abandon your baseless pride!
Love's fire burns my heart—
Bring wine in your lotus mouth!
                    —*Gita Govinda* 10.6[18]

   I don't know about you, but I think I would have sat up and paid more attention in my high school theology classes if we had used some of this material! This perfect marriage of unbridled sensuality and deep religious feeling is virtually unknown in our culture. It brings to mind the cry of the Gypsies and the wails and moans of the bluesmen, who let their music become a vehicle of love, a love that strives for a perfection that only comes when it can reach from the muck of earthly life to the purity of the spirit. In India, the lotus blossom, a flower of purity which commonly grows out of the mud, is the symbol for love, undefiled, miraculously rising out of this world of illusion.

   If perfect love is the goal, as it is for the Baul, their song and dance are the perfect vehicles for both the attainment of the goal and its communication:

   The songs form an indispensable part of Baul life
   . . . [they help him in his] eternal quest for the Man
   of the Heart and also these are the only ways to communicate his ideas to the ordinary men of the world.
   In short, the Baul does everything through his songs:
   he lives in his songs, he meditates in his songs, he
   sleeps in his songs, and he dies in his songs.
                    — R.M. Sarkar, *Bauls of Bengal: In Quest*
                    of the Man of the Heart [19]

The Baul's songs have a unique function: they literally form a link between heaven and earth, between the world of base passion and refined spiritual longing. Where did we come from? Where are we going? These questions can either engender feelings of awe and gratitude, or strike terror in our hearts. Now the vanished world we vaguely remember takes on a different meaning. Homesickness enters a metaphysical dimension.

Like the Gypsies and the blues players, many Bauls suffered indignities in their past. They escaped the crushing weight of Indian social convention by taking to the road with their drums and *dotaras* (small, lute-like instruments). Like the African Americans, they were not in a position to gain anything from mainstream society. They could not heal the wounds that almost inevitably happen to all of us, but they found in their wounds a doorway to something else. Like other fringe groups, Bauls have been led by circumstances of life to look beyond the superficialities of hidebound tradition to something deeper and more lasting. They are individuals who have chosen to take their deep dissatisfaction with ordinary life and do something creative with it: they use this inner tension for a life of discovery, creativity and service. Their goal is to transform the heat of suffering into the fire of passionate engagement with whatever life has to offer. All the practices of their life are built around this aim. What many men and women attempt to do instinctually through art, service or religion, the Baul does consciously through a life comprised of all three.

There is a story about a certain tribe of Gypsies in Egypt. When they first arrived in town they were scorned, accused of thievery, magic and begging for a living. Having no other recourse, and recognizing their greatest talent, they decided to conquer the hearts of the people through their music. Their word for this, *hawasiz*, literally means "invaders of the heart." Through the gift of their arts, the tribe was able to assimilate into the local society, and remained there for hundreds of years.

The music of the African Americans has certainly served a similar function: deprived for centuries of the most basic rights and opportunities, their music has invaded the hearts of our country and helped open the door to a more humane and dignified dialogue between the races. The Bauls as well have used their music to communicate who they are, and through that to give something to the larger community.

The Bauls call their way of life *sahaja*, which means natural and spontaneous, so it follows that music is one of the means by which they achieve their aim of transforming earthly suffering into divine longing.

> To them, spontaneous human feelings such as lust, anger and greed were to be understood as qualitative degrees of the same energy that gives rise to positive emotions such as love, generosity, and caring. Rather than reject or repress the destructive emotions, the [Bauls] sought to harness their power and transform them into a harmonious flow of positive energy. They composed many songs that expressed [this] . . .
>
> — Bhaskar Bhattacharya[20]

Like the primeval shamans, the wandering bluesmen and the charismatic preachers, music for the Bauls is their primary source of communication of a healing force that transcends the ordinary world—an all-consuming love that burns up everything in its path. Yet, the thought of annihilation in love that can bring tears to a Baul's eyes would make another person shudder in horror.

Communicating their teachings through music is a means of bypassing the rational mind and transmitting its salutary effects directly to the body, for music reaches far beyond the pale limit of words.

Bauls considered their songs sacred because they are a vehicle to take us beyond the mundane world, beyond our superficial psychological problems to an extraordinary reality where personality disappears and bare essence comes to the fore. Here there is only one "problem," the assumed separation between oneself and others, oneself and the universe, oneself and God. I say *assumed* because it is the primary human delusion that we are separate and distinct from the rest of creation. That assumption has fueled humans to build huge empires at great human cost. It has allowed war, slavery, and destruction of the earth to continue unabated. If one cause could be named for every problem that plagues mankind, it is this: that we act for our own good over and above (and often at the sacrifice of) the good of others. This is the disease the Baul attempts to eradicate through his unconventional lifestyle.

> And I revel only in the gladness of my own welling
>   love.
> In love there's no separation, but commingling
>   always,
> So I rejoice in song and dance with each and all.
>   —Nara-hari[21]

Baul performance is first and foremost a joyous affair of the heart, but, at the same time, it is quite serious. The songs are arrows of love meant to pierce the armor of the selfish ego and all its defenses, cutting straight to the raw, primal suffering of the illusion of separation. The Baul confronts this pain, lives with it, allows it to tenderize him or her—this is their path to transformation.

Baul's don't believe in searching for God outside daily life; rather, they hold that our experience in each moment is the thread that leads us to a more profound life. An ordinary experience can turn extraordinary simply by finding a way to make each action a prayer. For them, religion that attempts to artificially constrict our natural human passions is not only ineffective, but it denigrates the divine nature within us.

If God is worth celebrating at all, he must be approachable from wherever we are living in the moment, even if it's down in the muck. There are many stories of Jesus and other notable saints from diverse traditions preferring to keep company with common people, even outcasts. Those that had no place in society and were mired in sin were often much more receptive to esoteric teachings than those who were comfortably entrenched in the political establishment, like the Pharisees, who were too full of their own ideas and attached to their power to hear what Jesus was saying. Similarly, the Bauls, while scorned by the establishment, are nevertheless loved by the common people, because they bring the life of the spirit down to earth within everyone's grasp.

On the Road With the Bauls

The Bauls' passionate music, love for humanity, and urge for spiritual transformation comes across powerfully in their performances. In 1991, a group of three Bauls toured the western U.S., and I was lucky enough to catch them at the public library (of all places!) in the small town where I live.

Sanatan Das Baul, the leader of the group, is a small but imposing man of seventy. A bright power quietly radiated from beneath his orange patchwork robes, the traditional dress of the Baul. (They hand-make their clothing out of scraps of cloth from discarded items from both Muslims and Hindus, as a metaphor for their view of a religion that embraces all paths.) His two sons, Bishwanath and Basudeb, elegantly dressed up to their carefully wrapped turbans, were quiet and self-possessed, constantly looking to their father for direction. Sanatan Das Baul was a guru, and they were his disciples.

Their performance of music, dance and sung poetry that afternoon at the library was a sacred event for them, and they approached it with all the intensity, commitment and devotion one would expect. Despite their quiet reserve, I could feel an intensity from them, as if an inner fire blazed inside them. That "heat" drew people in, but it also made them shy away in fear of getting singed.

The Bauls started without fanfare; their first tentative taps on their drums fell almost randomly it seemed, and caught one's attention offguard. Sanatan Das Baul began to dance, ever so slowly, his ankle bells jangling as he moved in a circular pattern. As he picked up his bare feet and placed them down on the floor, I felt sure that nobody had ever done this with so much intention and force. Notes were plucked out of their *dotaras* almost as an afterthought, a melody taking shape with excruciating hesitation. These guys knew how to lay behind the beat! Every movement, gesture and sound was conspiring to create an appetite, a slowly kindling desire—a musical foreplay of staggering dimensions. Without any egoic display whatsoever, they riveted the attention of everyone in the room. In fact, they seemed almost oblivious of their audience, totally immersed in their music, enacting an eternal play of man's love for the divine. Yet, at the same time, their attitude did not turn anyone off to their charms. If they didn't acknowledge our presence, they also didn't seem to recognize their own—as if there was no one in the room at all.

Now, the audience's attention sufficiently caught in their web of sound, movement and mood, the musicians proceeded to shamelessly wail and cry out their songs of unattainable love. The language was of course completely unintelligible to me, as they sang in Bengali, yet the communication was clear. Even the English translation of the lyrics, which appeared in the program, seemed way off from what I was "hearing." Who could possibly translate these ancient, anguished prayers, these love songs offered to an unreachable object of desire? These sentiments came from a place no words could touch, a wound no words could heal, a conflagration of adoration that nothing could survive. The lyrics were there just to dazzle the mind and keep it entertained, while the heart was roasted alive.

The Bauls illuminated a model of life that was both inspiring and approachable, radiating the incandescence of the spirit in a very human setting. With their every gesture, they communicated the richness of simplicity of their lives. They are beggar kings.

For weeks after this moving performance I felt the impact of this music in my own heart. I realized once again how many people in the West hunger for a life that is more solidly rooted in the things of the earth and enjoyment of the body, a more passionate way of living. Many of us, myself included, have forgotten how to be fed by simple things—a walk, a meal shared with friends, conversation, silence. An amazing depth of nourishment is available to us when we can allow ourselves to be touched by life. And while we need to ground ourselves in the simple things, I think we also yearn for a spiritual tradition that honors the mystical urge within each of us, and affirms the possibility of contacting God here and now, in this body, not in some hazy afterlife to come. Love of God, love of ordinary life: the Bauls, more than any other group of which I'm aware, embrace these polarities with equanimity and grace. Akin to the ancient shamans— the master magicians with one foot set firmly in each world—the dance of the Bauls simultaneously sets the stars trembling and the earth shaking. Before Christopher Columbus and Neil Armstrong, these musical magicians were the true voyagers, drawing out worlds within worlds through sacred chants and rhythms.

For the Bauls, music is a reminder to live our lives with joy, gratitude and acceptance. Music is not only about pleasing the ear; it's about creating deeper relationship between people. In fact, music *is* relationship; without this lived connection with oneself and others, melodies become meaningless strings of notes, rhythms become purposeless patterns, dance becomes heartless posturing, words fall flat at the audience's feet. Authentic expression is about losing interest in impressing others or even pleasing them aesthetically; it's about calling people to join the dance of life. When we touch our true nature, what naturally arises is an intoxicating longing to be overwhelmed by a spiritual presence. We want to succumb to our own source.

Maybe this power of music to awaken us to our essential nature is why the Hindus (among others) believe that sound as vibration is the essence of the universe, and it alone existed before everything else came into being through it. John Coltrane acknowledged this when he made his album entitled *Om*, which is the sacred syllable Hindus believe is at the source of creation. Coltrane was an avid student of all religions, and consciously sought to embody spiritual principles in his performance, composition and daily life. Nevertheless, he never lost sight of the blues, the all-too-human roots of his music. Many jazz players have remarked that their music loses something vital when it gets too far away from its humble beginnings.

Coltrane's flights into musical/mystical ecstasy were not taken at the expense of the nitty gritty details of human life, and neither are those of the Bauls. When one journeys into the heart of creation itself (and it seems that some artists have been gifted with the ability to take their art form to that level, a level that transcends the form) one doesn't leave behind the blues; they simply take on a different meaning.

Bengali blues is about hitting a metaphysical bottom, losing all hope, falling into the void. It is knowing the unquenchable thirst of desire, the heart that encompasses all space that can never be filled. Our desires and passions are all but threads to a yearning that has no possibility of fulfillment in this world, a yearning that can pull us beyond hope and fear, if we dare to fall into it. The message of the Bauls is that, ultimately, our heartache is not personal.

In The Beginning Was the Blues . . .

While we're on the subject of India, I am reminded of a Hindu creation story that aptly describes what I would call the cosmic blues. (Remember Janis Joplin's "Kosmic Blues Band?")

In the beginning God alone existed. He was called Shiva. As he was reflecting on himself he suddenly became afraid. But then Shiva thought, "Why should I be frightened, since I alone exist?" At that point Shiva experienced loneliness, and he desired company. He proceeded to create a female companion for himself, the Goddess Shakti. They sported together in cosmic marital bliss.

One day (assuming Shiva had by now created time of course), Shakti realized, "I am being intimate with the Lord, yet I have been created out of his own body." Feeling shame about this, she changed herself into a cow to hide from Shiva. But Shiva found her out. Changing himself into a bull he mated with her, creating the entire race of bulls. Shakti then changed herself into a ewe, but Shiva changed himself into a ram. He mated with her again, creating the race of rams. As you can imagine, this went on for a long time, until the entire world was created.

When I found this myth, I was struck with how perfectly it fit into the "blues cosmology." What if the universe wasn't created out of some perfect divine plan? Life often seems like some kind of accident borne out of loneliness and desire, so why not the universe itself? One could say that the people who concocted this story were just projecting their own human emotions on God. Yet, the experience of heartache and longing is so universal that if it is true that we are made in God's image, why not say: "In the beginning there was only God, existing alone within an endless void. He had the blues . . ."

You may wonder what business an ancient Hindu myth has in a book about the blues. Truth is, the blues thrives on myth, its lyrics abound in myths. What about the story of the seventh son with magical powers who can heal the sick and raise the dead? Or the woman whose lovin' is so good it can make a blind man see and a dumb man talk? And don't forget all the mojos and goofer dust either. An authentic tradition is sustained by the life-giving powers of mythology, for myth raises our ordinary experience to a higher level beyond the personal. Myths not only show that every man and woman on the face of the earth has had the same kinds of experiences, but more importantly, it shows that our experience is rooted in something divine, even if it was a divine accident.

One may argue, "But those myths came from the people who created the tradition in the first place? You can't just add in anything you feel like." That's true, yet the tradition is not static. Being a living entity, a tradition changes constantly, sheds old skin, learns new tricks. The blues has obviously gone through many changes in the last hundred years, and far from being hurt from those changes, it is still here, strong as ever. That's the key to getting what the music has to offer, realizing that by playing and listening to the blues, we are taking part in a tradition, one that can serve us tremendously if we respect it and care for it. I don't think, however, that caring for the tradition means fossilizing old playing styles and creating rigid boundaries about what is and isn't authentic blues. If we think we are personally responsible for being the custodians of the tradition, that is just musical hubris. The tradition itself decides where it is going, and what new myths are going to serve those who are serving it.

Shri's Eastern Blues

I can't explain it, but I do hear a connection between the blues and Eastern music. Jimmy Page of Led Zeppelin has heard the same thing: "I saw a parallel between the bending of guitar strings in blues music, and the emotional quality of that, with what was being done in Indian music."[22] Check out the Paul Butterfield Blues Band's album entitled *East/West* if you don't believe American blues and Indian ragas share an emotional resonance. Indian musicians also bend the notes to achieve various moods; and like the blues, their music has complex, multi-layered rhythms. It's no accident that the blues revival in the sixties, which saw scores of English and American bands covering traditional blues songs, coincided with an interest in Indian music by these same artists. As Page says, the parallel is on a level of feeling.

In 1993 Shri was still a young band, and we didn't have any fixed ideas about what the blues was supposed to sound like. For a few months I had been holding onto some lyrics from Lee that really struck me, a song called *Blind Devotion*. These lyrics were unlike anything I had ever seen or heard before in a popular song; the profundity and tenderness they communicated was more akin to Persian love poetry than the blues or rock and roll. I had to find music for these words that cried out for expression.

One day I was fooling around with a different tuning on my guitar, one which is nearly identical to the way an Indian sitar is tuned (and, oddly enough, it is also a very common tuning for Celtic music). The tuning allows one to keep a note constantly droning while the melody is played on top, just like in Indian music. As I played, a haunting melody began to take shape, and I realized that *Blind Devotion* would not be a typical blues song, but something more like an Eastern chant. It reminded me of early blues songs which, instead of having chord changes, create a trancelike pulse with a single chord and a simple melody. Those songs sound a lot like chants, fresh from their transformation from sung prayers and field hollers to the form we know today.

Our song *Blind Devotion* is one that bridges thousands of miles and countless years in the territory it covers. Some songs come out smooth and easy; others are a protracted labor—in the middle of the process I wanted to forget the whole thing ever happened. *Blind Devotion* was one of those difficult births. Deborah and I worked on it for weeks. We'd have something figured out, and then one of us would come into practice and change it, infuriating the other. (We walked out on practice more than once.) Only the transcendent quality of the lyrics kept us going, working together through all obstacles.

When we finally worked out the arrangement and performed *Blind Devotion* for the first time, we knew we had something very special. At first, the Eastern melodies and rhythm take people by surprise, but soon they're swooning in the transcendence of the words. After five years, *Blind Devotion* is still the song we are most proud of. Its mysterious power enchants audiences, and because of that we only play it as an encore, when the mood is right. Many people have asked us who wrote this song, as if they had a hazy memory of hearing it somewhere a long time ago.

> Ask me to do anything
> your wish is my command
> I will fly up to the sun for you
> bring it to your hand
> I will conquer armies

you know what I mean
Allow me to adore you
be your slave, not your queen

Got a question for you honey
please forgive my great emotion
Is it dangerous to love you
with such blind devotion

Fingers intertwined, paroxysm of love
that is my idea of praying
lost in your lover so deeply
you don't even know what you're saying
don't know much about the subject of holy
but I think I have come pretty near
when I'm looking deep into his eyes
there I am transfixed with fear

Blind devotion, what else is left
nothing that is worth very much
Blind devotion, consume me in your path
let me feel the heaven and sorrow
of your touch

Got a question for you honey
please forgive my great emotion
Is it dangerous to love you
with such blind devotion[23]

I remember one hot and sultry July afternoon, Shri was playing
in Prescott's town square, directly across from the County

Courthouse steps. People were sitting all along the steps and in the grass under trees, avoiding the wide-open space right in front of the stage because of the unrelenting Arizona sun. I love playing in these situations because I get to see people of all ages responding to our music, and I think of Johnny Shines saying how the blues don't have no age, no race, no class. That afternoon everybody was digging the sound—couples in their seventies were dancing together right next to groups of teenagers who stood there being cool, watching intently. We decided to end the set with *Blind Devotion.*

Just as the first notes resounded, three middle-aged men came into the space only twenty feet or so in front of the stage. It was impossible to overlook their presence, because there was no one else anywhere near them, and they were completely intent on what we were doing. One of the men was in a wheelchair, and another had a bad limp. All three looked pretty ragged in their torn jeans and bandannas.

The moment I saw them, I don't know how, but I knew they were Vietnam veterans. They had that look of too much experience; of being burned out, raw. They sat there like statues, taking it all in, and as I watched them I felt like we were intimately connected, that we were all part of some mysterious, timeless ritual. Tears came to my eyes as I sensed the tremendous pain that their difficult lives had wrought upon their hearts. I saw the sadness of the world in that moment, and I felt this song acting as a healing balm to those in need, every one of us. How mysterious, I thought, that I could read the hearts of these men whom I had never seen before in my life. A tremendous desire arose in me—one could only call it a prayer—to use this music to ease the suffering of the world. In that moment, I knew it was possible.

Chapter 6

Sex, Blues and Rock and Roll

The blues is about a woman.
                    —Sam Chatmon[1]

The blues is not a dream; the blues is truth.
                    —Brownie McGhee[2]

Supposing truth is a woman—what then?
                    —Friedrich Nietzche[3]

Sex and the blues have always been intimate partners. Before the sexual revolution of the 1960s (which was largely fueled by the in-your-face eroticism of rock and roll) blues and jazz singers had been spelling out the facts of life for over fifty years. In the 1920s and '30s, Bessie Smith was singing about lesbianism and wanting her man to go "deep sea diving." The blues uses every possible metaphor for sex one could imagine: squeezing lemons, fishing ponds, roosters crowing, cows being milked, and of course, jelly rolls, a fascinating metaphor because it is the only word I know of that can refer to both the male and female genitalia. Now that's economy of language!

It is through the blues that Legba, the mischievous African god, returns, standing proud with penis erect and primed to explode. At the entrance to many African villages, it is common to see an image of an ithyphallic god, ready to greet newcomers with his magnanimous erection, reminding all of the power of creation that is both terrifying and blissful. Yes, the god who gains our entry into the spirit worlds is also the god who delights in wreaking chaos upon us poor humans, and what easier domain to achieve that in than the domain of sex. Legba, almost lost when blacks turned to the Christian Church, has survived many indignities: he survived the difficult sea voyage to the new world; he survived slavery and segregation; he survived the dirt-poor sharecropper's shack and the crumbling inner city. The spirit of the African god was preserved through those primeval bluesmen, whose sexual desire was frightening in its intensity. Legba remains because he lives in the music.

And the blues brings back the great earth goddess too. The round, fertile woman with huge breasts has been worshipped for eons as the bringer of fertility (for both humans and crops) and marital and social harmony. It is good to remember that the ideal feminine archetype of early tribal cultures was the opposite of our current ideal female. This earth goddess archetype is found in the blues in personalities like Ma Rainey, Big Mama Thornton, Etta James and Aretha Franklin: big, powerful women whose voices could level buildings. When we see women like these sing—how they command a space; how they effortlessly communicate the softness and sensuality of essential femininity; how they are absolutely rooted in the earth; how their presence and magnetism burn hotter than the hottest stage lights—when we can see these women for who they truly are, then we know there is something wrong with the way this culture views women. The great earth goddess is not worshipped for how glamorous she looks, but for how much raw feminine energy and vital sexual power she holds.

Tribal religions everywhere are full of sexual imagery; often, male and female sex organs are worshipped for their creative, life-giving powers. But it should be understood that these images don't refer to our human genitalia, but rather the cosmic genitalia, in whose image ours are made (they left that part out of Genesis). Healthy sex is guaranteed when people know that the sexual act is a mirror image of the cosmic creative principle, that one's partner is literally a conduit for the energy that feeds the universe.

The healing of the breakdown of relations between men and women won't happen with achieving greater and greater sexual and emotional freedom, for those issues are just symptomatic of a larger problem, namely that we cannot see the opposite sex as shining facets of the original divine man or woman. When the cultural institutions that are supposed to delineate the sacred fail to inform us of the profoundly spiritual aspects of our sexuality, we cannot help but treat our partner with less than the respect they deserve. How we long, in this culture, for a return to this way of seeing things; yet how clumsy and infantile are our attempts to recreate this relationship to sacred sexuality. We worship the earth goddess as a skinny super-model in slinky underwear—we pay her millions for her services, but nevertheless have denied her essential nature.

Every once in a while, however, I see our music create a difference in how women are seen or see themselves. A few years ago we played in Payson, nestled in the high country of Arizona, where the high desert spotted with scrub bushes meets the edge of the dark, pine forested mountains. Pete's Place was a rickety wooden building right off the highway a few miles outside of town. Ancient well-loved pick-ups were parked side by side with their more recent, sleeker incarnations. When we walked into the bar we were greeted with strains of Tammy Wynette over the jukebox, a quick perusal of which revealed that they liked *both* kinds of music in this place: country *and* western. Sawdust covered the floor, and a sea of black and white cowboy hats surrounded the bar. I half expected someone to drag some farm animals through the room at any moment. Fear gripped me as

I realized that we were deep in the heart of cowboy country, and I wondered who in the hell booked this gig.

As we were setting up, an older man with a weathered face sauntered up to the stage. "What kinda music y'all play?" the words dripping out of his mouth in a thick drawl.

"Oh, a little bit of everything," I blurted out, then muttered, "Well, mostly blues."

"Sounds good. Know any Patsy Cline?"

"No, sorry."

"Well, you and the little ladies be sure to give us a good time tonight!"

"You bet!"

I shot a look of "What the hell are we doing here?" at Deborah, who immediately responded with an expression of, "I have no fucking idea!"

As starting time approached, the bar gradually filled to capacity, a down-home hootin' and hollerin' crowd ready for a party. I was relieved to see quite a few women (our ever-sympathetic audience) filling the tables near the stage. We knew we could not be tentative at all in a situation like this, so we kicked into our strongest material, with a message women anywhere could relate to.

> You said you'd love me until you die
> Don't make promises you can't keep
> You said you would never ever make me cry
> Don't make promises that you can't keep
>
> One day positive, the next day not
> Talk's just words, just words . . .
>
> —*Don't Make Promises*[4]

Shukyo was drumming with the force of a locomotive, Tina moving with feminine grace and sensuousness, and Deborah unabashedly exuding the raw force of woman itself, strutting her stuff, singing the secret desires of her heart, singing the sad and beautiful story of all women everywhere. Her elegant grace and simple gestures flowed out from the source of truth. She was not afraid to bare her broken heart, but she didn't flaunt it either. For Deborah, sharing her intimate feelings is not a badge of honor, nor a plea for attention; it just arises naturally from her relationship with the audience.

The crowd of mostly women was soon up on their feet and kickin' up some serious sawdust. The men at the bar seemed to shrink in size as their little women were furiously shakin' and pushin' their hips to the music, smiles on their faces as they took in these words

Deborah lavishes her smile on the audience.

which affirmed who they were and what they felt in their most intimate places. Between sets, one disconcerted man confided in me (a little suspicious about my complicity in these matters):

"Looks like we got a full fledged women's support group on this dance floor."

I responded with all the laconic cowboy wit I could muster: "Yep, sure does."

Actually, after a while many of the men looked past their fear and noticed how attractive these women had become. Soon many of the men were out on the dance floor as well, unknowingly drinking up the atmosphere of juicy abandon. Many women walked up to Deborah, Tina, and Heather after the show and thanked them with such sincerity for their extraordinary genuineness. They said things like, "You made me feel so good about myself." As opposed to all the attention in this culture on glamour, self-improvement and having it all together, the women in Shri take a straightforward and refreshing approach to life. Their willingness to be perfectly ordinary, to not try to appear any more than who they are, really inspires the women in our audiences.

That night I learned another lesson about the universality of the blues, about never underestimating the music's power to obliterate all the distinctions we make between people. I have met some individuals who did not care for the music, but I have not yet run across any strata of society that doesn't relate to it in some way. At the end of the night, one older couple came up to us and said enthusiastically, "We've never heard this music before. We like the blues!"

Teenage Blues

Because we have forgotten the true functions of men and women in relationship to each other, puberty can be a hellish time for many in

139

this culture. No wonder the onset of hormonal changes signals massive confusion. I was no exception. When I turned fourteen I definitely had the blues, although at that time I wouldn't have used those words. Just as puberty hit and the mystery of woman began to assert itself rather insistently into my consciousness, I started at a new school—an all-male, Jesuit, Catholic training ground with decidedly anti-sexual undertones. When all I was interested in was the curves and contours and secret places of women's bodies, I was swept up into an ivory tower of the mind, where morality and discipline were the new gods. I was experiencing all kinds of strange and powerful feelings, but they were virtually ignored by those who were supposed to be the wise elders of society. Why was this passion and yearning unleashed into my unsuspecting body only to be thwarted by puritanical elitists? My four high-school years were filled with frustration, confusion and depression.

Coincidentally, around this time I also discovered the power of rock and roll. Music was my savior. While Jesus (or, more accurately, my teachers' distorted version of him) beckoned me to a life of moral uprightness (and uptightness) devoid of magic and feeling, rock and roll presented a brand new and much more appealing pantheon of gods. At the time, Led Zeppelin was my favorite group. They dabbled in realms of myth and mysticism, blending blues, rock, Celtic and Eastern music into an emotionally and sexually supercharged sound. I spent countless hours after school listening to their music; lying on my bed with eyes closed, I entered a meditative world where all the feelings that were denied to me during the long school day were allowed free reign.

Many musicians and music lovers attest that hearing certain music literally turned their lives around and gave them hope to get through bleak adolescent ordeals. Eric Clapton said that:

. . . through most of my youth my back was against the wall and the only way to survive that was with dignity and pride and courage . . . I heard that most of all in the blues. It was [about] one guy who was completely alone and had no options and no alternatives whatsoever other than to just sing and play to ease his pain . . . that echoed what I felt.[5]

In my adolescence, rock and roll and the blues served the same function: the music kept me connected to myself, allowed me to stay real, to acknowledge my body, to remember that my feelings were important to me, despite the barrage of messages to the contrary. In this sense the blues and rock and roll are alike: they are both protest music, affirmations of aspects of the human spirit that many in this culture would prefer to ignore or even wipe out altogether.

The Blues is a Woman

The first time I met the blues was in 1986, when I was seventeen— I saw Stevie Ray Vaughan perform in New York City, in one of those jaw-dropping shows. Stevie Ray, a man possessed by an unrelenting inner fire, played almost nonstop for two hours without letting up the energy for one moment. His fingers, entirely fluent in the arcana of the blues, were like furious bees gathering the nectar of song. Like Jimi Hendrix, he seemed to torture sounds out of his guitar, obsessed with squeezing out every ounce of unexpressed feeling within himself. It seemed to me that the higher he went the more yearning he had to hit that ineluctable, indefinable state, to simply become a rushing torrent of sound/feeling, to shout his whole purpose as a human being in one unparalleled note. I was unprepared for this man's intensity, for nothing in rock and roll had ever touched me like this before.

That night was the beginning of my conversion to blues music. I saw that the blues was about knowing one's heart, knowing it so deeply that it becomes the music itself. I knew then that the art is in the feeling. To be oneself sincerely is to automatically invoke the living tradition. For me, the challenge is always to make the same three chords and six-note scale say a million things, to express the precise feeling of each unique moment. Only total dedication to the inner voice will do. Those who spend countless hours memorizing licks may sound smooth, but they're missing the number one rule of the blues: it's a "soul thang."

That night Stevie brought me his gospel, a traveling prayer meeting in a battered guitar case. To witness someone like him play is to understand why some bluesmen have slept with their guitars beside them in their beds. For them, nothing is more faithful and more precious than the blues, their constant friend and protector, their shelter from always impinging troubles. The blues is not just *about* a woman, it *is* a woman.

To see Stevie bleed his guitar dry; to hear Muddy's voice booming out over his infamous Chicago blues beat; to hear Fred McDowell's haunting slide guitar; to hear the real blues is to be immersed in the mystery of woman, because this music, like woman, soothes and consoles our restless soul (both women's and men's). It is a conduit through which pure feminine presence can flow into our world. All the elements of music that ignite passionate obsession in the music lover have their counterparts in woman, and good music is equivalent to making love: with the band, with the audience and with one's instrument.

To make musical love, everyone in the band has to be in the right mood, a mood we could call surrender. When the band hits the elusive groove, that mysterious eternal moment when the rhythm just rolls over us (a moment which is sought after by musicians and lovers alike), then each player begins to coax sounds out of their instruments with delight, just as lovers caress each other, listening for that delicate sigh that signals that the heat is rising. The beat of all music originates from the primal rhythms of love-making, whether they be rockin' and rollin' or smooth and sultry.

When the blues are coming on strong and the music is hitting that tender spot inside, we can almost be sure there's a woman involved (or, in the case of a woman performer, a man—I'll stick to my point of view purely for ease of style). I may be thinking of a particular woman, but she is also just a front for a more archetypal feminine presence. When her image shimmers before me, calling, the notes I play are steeped in the sap of desire, showering down like crimson rain. Every note, every movement, every pause, every moment of frustration or completion—it's all about relationship with her. Looked at from one angle, my life can be seen as a gradual initiation into the mystery of woman; undulating waves of intense desire to jump into her followed by fear of the unknown worlds of feeling that reside within her and within myself. The fascination of entering a woman physically belies a deeper desire: to enter her spiritually, which is really to enter *myself* in a whole new way.

Playing the blues is a great way for me to explore this territory, and the more courage I can muster to really go exploring, the more the music benefits. It feels as if there's a bottomless well of unfulfilled passion within me—the longing practically plays itself. Sometimes anger arises from the pain of feeling alone—rage bursts forth from the guitar, bombarding the club with staccato bullets of sound. Other times, playing guitar comes as close as possible to making love onstage as decorum allows, as its sounds become gentle caresses, moans of desire, passionate thrusts, sighs of ecstasy. The guitar becomes either a woman's body or an extension of my own. It becomes a power object, a vehicle for traveling into the world of feeling, of sexuality, a world that seemed like forbidden territory to me because of my religious upbringing. A rich night of playing can encompass my life history of relationship, and it even has the power to rewrite the story, or at least add a new chapter.

The first time something like this happened to me, the energy present onstage was out of control, like suddenly getting plugged into a 220-volt socket. One night we were playing Albert King's, *Born Under a Bad Sign*, a song where I typically take a long solo. That night Deborah and I, as usual, were playfully egging each other on to go for it in our performance. On this song, Deborah hit a new height, singing with unparalleled ferocity, digging deep for the place in her that feels the truth of the lyrics. Not only did she get there, she dragged everyone else in the club with her. We all felt like we were "born under a bad sign," as if God had created a special thirteenth Zodiac sign just to make life miserable. I could remember those moments when I felt utterly crushed by life's indifference, and I could sense the gratitude in the audience for Deborah's courage to go to that place and sing that utter despair, no holds barred.

Now I was truly fired up. As soon as I launched into my solo, it was like falling through a door into another space that had been waiting there all along. I was playing from all the hopelessness I had ever felt in my life, trying to play out of that dark place, to arrive somewhere else. There was no separation between myself and the guitar. With my eyes closed, almost completely unaware of the audience or even the rest of the band, I suddenly went beyond playing "notes." I was wildly using the whammy bar and "wah-wah" pedal, just making sounds, like a child cooing and screaming simply for the joy of finding his own voice. Falling to my knees, my whole body violently swayed as the stagelights and sound pulsated in my head.

The next thing that happened was unexpected—I became

enraged at all the people from my past whom I felt had encouraged me to cut myself off from my feeling life, my sexuality, my heart. But I wasn't just thinking it—I was moving and writhing and using the guitar as a talisman to direct my long-repressed bitter rage, lost in a world of feeling I never knew existed. Now, still kneeling, I was arched back so that my head was actually touching the floor. The guitar was part of my body, absolutely. It was my voice—not my intellectual voice, but the voice of my pain and rage and anguish and despair. My guitar became a battering ram out of the prison that was my body, the body which is shackled from the inside—not the body I was born with, but the body that *they* made for me so that I could fit into *their* dead world, a world where there's no air, no speech, no freedom, no spontaneous yelling out of who I am for no reason except that I exist, I am here, and I'm happy. That moment was not simply about cutting free of the past—it was out of time . . . from my real self that has always existed . . . a cry from the world of the wounded heart, the crippled emotions. I felt as if some great master had just invisibly walked through the room, proclaiming, "Rise, and know that you are not dead!" Hallelujah! When we finished the song I knew I had been traveling in another world, and my body was trembling from all the energy that was unleashed. The rest of the gig was permeated by a heightened sense of intimacy with the rest of the band. I remember looking over at Tina and sharing a smile, suddenly able to take in and appreciate her, and what she was offering, more than ever. Releasing my demons had the added benefit of releasing my fear of being close to people.

These magical moments have happened many times for us in Shri. Some nights, we'll walk onstage in severe states of internal turmoil, not speaking to each other and avoiding eye contact, and I'm wondering how on earth we're going to get through the gig without a fight breaking out and someone walking offstage, when suddenly there's the music and the only thing to do is to play my anger, my sadness, my pain, and as I'm pouring all this feeling into the guitar, and Deborah is pouring her's into her singing, we're realizing that the music sounds great, the crowd is into it, and suddenly, mysteriously, we're . . . we're happy! How did that happen? Pain and despair literally transformed into elation within a mere hour or two! It has definitely been cause for reflection about what this music really is.

Music, particularly the blues, invites us to address our suffering in a way that does not cave into our pain, but instead uses it to open up to relationship and healing. We've commonly had people in the audience tell us things like, "I was having such a bad day before I came here tonight, but now I can't even remember what I was upset about. Your music totally changed my mood." Or: "My husband and I had a terrible fight, but after hearing you guys play I'm gonna go home and make up with him." When we go beyond the music and play the "blues" inside us, we unleash this miraculous power to transform our darkness into light: pain turns into compassion; anger melts into passionate joy; lonely lust brightens into ecstatic longing; self-pity opens into gratitude; despair bursts into hope and faith. Playing the blues has shown me that the emotions I habitually avoided all my life (because society taught me they were "bad") can be turned into saving graces.

Needless to say, when anyone in the band gets into a state like that, people come up to us after the set with beaming smiles, thanking us effusively. There is a healing exchange that happens when we allow the music to transform our pain into inspiration, for those who come to listen also feel this need for release. This is the mercurial power of music: the blues performer has the gift of resonance, the ability to strike the same feeling in the hearts of many, just as a tuning fork begins to vibrate sympathetically when it's signature note is played. He or she can make people feel, and that is why they come.

A French man I met in a club told me that he liked all music, but the only music he *loved* was blues. "I would travel anywhere in the world for it." When I asked him why, he said, "Because it makes me feel." As he said this he gestured with his hands, his fists closed, pulling them back and forth across his stomach. It gave me the impression of an inner tension that only felt release through this music that he loved. He approached the music in the same way I did, to work him over from the inside out.

Our personal struggles enacted through music can touch people in surprising ways. When we are able to communicate parts of ourselves that we had hidden behind closed doors for years, the act of freeing ourselves in the moment and in front of an audience can have electrifying effects. Others are inspired to do the same. There is a powerful, sympathetic resonance between performer and audience—one spark onstage can ignite the whole room, and the conflagration can build on itself indefinitely. When we are subsumed by that fire we suddenly know each other like never before, as if our real selves needed to be cooked to a certain temperature before they could truly take form. The blues is my favorite way of cooking up some soul.

Stepping onstage can be an opportunity to drop the mask that I live with all the time, the mask that separates me from myself as well as others. That demonic guitar solo during *Bad Sign* was a chance for me to drop my pretense of being the nice guy who doesn't feel any pain, and get into what was really going on for me. The tendency in our society is to mask our pain, but performance is about reversing that process, letting it all hang out. Playing the blues with Shri has led me to see that I don't have to do anything special to be who I am; I just have to stop hiding.

For me, the most inspiring performers are those who can drop all masks and pretense, exposing themselves naked and raw, completely vulnerable. But it's not just about performance. Hopefully, when I've contacted a deeper part of myself onstage, I can allow that experience to permeate my daily life, instead of pretending it never happened.

The Birth of the White Man's Blues

It was just like the day Jesus walked on earth—that's the way that music was. It just had to happen . . .
    —Charlie Feathers, founding father of Rockabilly.[6]

It is impossible to talk about how the blues has impacted American society in this century (especially with regard to its attitude about sex) without mentioning rock and roll, since that was the way that most of us first encountered the blues. In the first two decades of rock and roll, blues and blues-inspired songs formed the repertoire of many major artists, from Elvis Presley to Janis Joplin to the Allman Brothers. And even into the nineties, blues songs were still cropping up in unexpected places, continuing to breathe vitality and simple, honest feeling into all kinds of music. It was listening to these blues-inspired rock and rollers that eventually turned me on to the "straight and natch'l blue."

Rock and roll was the result of a collision of cultures—a Western European culture that valued ideas above all else, and an African body-centered culture that valued the feeling life of the body. At the time, this marriage of black and white music that engendered rock and roll was shrouded in secrecy, a forbidden union in the red-light district of American culture. Like all taboo acts, it incited a desire that broke the boundaries of conventional tastes, and the shudders of ecstasy that followed rippled across the nation. Suddenly, the pent-up feelings of an entire generation were being nationally broadcast, as Elvis gyrated on The Ed Sullivan Show. The veils were being lifted—soon all hell would break loose.

As Muddy Waters sang, "The blues had a baby and they called it rock and roll." It was the white man's blues, repackaged for the easily shocked sensibilities of the times. The blues was the devil's own music in the South, and rock and roll was its dark spawn, inciting the same outrage and indignation in the white community that the blues did in the black. In both cases, the offending factor was the same: sex.

> The reaction to rock and roll was immediate and bitter. In the south, many white groups recognized the strong Negro influence in the music and tried to suppress it. Police in several northern cities found that the emotional atmosphere was too much for many white teenagers and they had to ban rock and roll dances.
>
> — Samuel Charters, *The Country Blues* [7]

A newsletter from a Minneapolis Catholic Youth Center actually exhorted adolescents to ". . . smash the records you possess which present a pagan culture and a pagan way of life."[8]

Fortunately, the forces of repression couldn't hold back the bursting dam. The youth went crazy for this new mulatto beat, and plunged into the new gyrations and twists, the shakes and rattles and rolls. Young girls practically pulled their hair out screaming in ecstasy over some oversexed man on stage doing unimaginable things with his hips. This was extremely disconcerting for the elders of the time. Fifteen years of careful and strict childrearing, preparing the next generation of American youth to lead this great country into ever-increasing material progress, went down the tubes in a flash. One thrust of Elvis' pelvis and it was all over.

The transformation of rhythm and blues into rock and roll

unleashed a powerful and unexpected force into our culture. Bo Diddley, one of the great innovators of rock and roll, described what this force is:

> Guys kind of piss me off trying to name what I'm doing. A lot of times I tell people, I don't know what it is, I just play it. But I do know what it is. It's mixed up with spiritual, sanctified rhythms, and the feeling I put into it when I'm playing, I have the feeling of making people shout . . . If you can't lock them into that [shout] mode, they don't move.[9]

Now the southern black ecstatic church services were not only finding their way into the blues, but into a new music that the whole nation was hearing. People literally didn't know what hit them. German anthropologist Leo Frobenius documented this phenomenon earlier in this century when he dubbed the Africans the "Invisible Counterplayers" for their largely unrecognized influence on Western Europe, exploding the myth that cultural gifts only flowed in one direction. He stated, "I have no doubt that [the Africans] worked upon the [European] cultures, from the south."[10] This pattern played itself out in America as well, as the musical and spiritual gifts of simpler folk from the South gradually infiltrated and transformed many elements of American life.

It cannot be overstated that the birth of rock and roll was as much a watershed for American societal mores as any event in the twentieth century. Twenty-five hundred years ago, Plato stated in *The Republic* that changes in the mode of music would inevitably foreshadow changes in society, and that these should be avoided lest we imperil the delicate balance of the social structure. To put it more simply, as we stated earlier, music communicates worldview. The introduction of black music into mainstream society in the form of rock and roll did just what Plato said it would; it disrupted the social order. Much to almost everyone's amazement, this new music became the driving force behind a cultural revolution that inspired new ways of dancing and dress, greater sexual freedom, social protest, interest in mystical religions and drug experimentation. People's worldviews changed practically overnight. Rock music was unique in American and possibly all of world history for one reason: never before had the younger generation had such a powerful way to voice their thoughts and feelings. Rock and roll may be *the* American cultural icon.*

The power of rock and roll was due to the way in which it woke up our bodies. Michael Ventura wrote:

> The history of jazz and rock and roll . . . [tell] the story of how the American sense of the body changed and deepened in the twentieth century— how Americans began the slow, painful process, still barely started now, of transcending the mind-body split they'd inherited from European culture.[11]

The music addressed a pressing need: to simply experience, express and celebrate one's body in all its fullness, without censure from the community. Sexual repression was a natural outcome of the growing worship of the technocratic society, where dedication to work, progress, comfort, money and order were the guiding princi-

---

*It is ironic that, just as white music began to embody more tension, black music went in the other direction. As soon as blacks began to enter the middle class in the 1960s, and many doors that were previously shut tight to them began to open, a major change in the mode of black music followed right along: blacks dropped the downhearted blues melodies and started listening to soul music, which used happier sounding major scales, less dissonant intervals, and a more relaxed beat.

ples, and where enjoyment was what happened *after* you got all your work done. Rock and roll turned this philosophy on its head.

Got Those 1950s Blues

The story of rock and roll is really the story of the first time that middle-class American society dipped into the stream of African American culture in a significant way. The inception of the blues in white culture was about the 1950s' Americans recognizing on some level (albeit mostly unconsciously) that they indeed had the blues, that the earthy, tragic songs of the rural black South and urban ghettoes indeed expressed what they felt.

The modern progressive society in the 1950s was based on denial of its roots. Ever increasing material and psychological comfort was the goal. Scientific and technological progress was the new religion, the savior. Soon it would eliminate work, starvation, disease, and maybe even death itself. But until our eventual triumph over nature's evils, we all had to do our part to keep the great machine moving forward. That meant years of being schooled into the guiding principles of the age, as well as years of dedication to career. The idea that one's career might be fulfilling or even enjoyable was not a consideration. To participate in this great endeavor was to reap certain rewards, but there was also a price: our inner lives.

In truth, the great American experiment of unlimited technological progress is directly antagonistic to life as we have known it on earth for millions of years, because it is trying to control something that is intrinsically beyond our control: nature. Nearly every technological achievement we have made is a direct attempt to replace a natural process with a man-made one, or to manipulate or even eliminate some element of nature. The car eliminates walking; telephones eliminate talking face to face; radio and TV eliminate live performances; and soon computers may eliminate human contact and deep thinking altogether.

It is bad enough that we have cut ourselves off from a whole way of being in the physical world, but unfortunately it doesn't end there. As we cut ourselves off from our bodies, we also lose touch with the life of the soul—passion, sexuality, true feeling, longing and love. When we separate ourselves from discomfort, we also sacrifice lots of good stuff as well. Joy is a full-body experience, but if we aren't inhabiting our bodies we have little chance to feel it.

This culture continues to drift further and further away from a natural, relaxed and celebratory relationship to the body. From an early age, we are assaulted with thousands of hours of television images; our brains are becoming hardwired to an ever more pervasive imaginary electronic reality. But TV is not the only culprit. Jerry Mander, in *The Absence of the Sacred*, paints a vivid portrait of this technology-driven world:

> From morning to night we walk though a world that is totally manufactured, a creation of human invention. We are surrounded by pavement, machinery, gigantic concrete structures. Automobiles, airplanes, computers, appliances, television, electric lights, artificial air have become the physical universe with which our senses interact. They are what we touch, observe, react to . . . as we relate to these objects of our own creation, we begin to merge with them and assume some of their characteristics . . . [l]iving constantly inside an environment of our own invention, reacting solely to things we ourselves have created, we are essentially living inside our own minds.[12]

What does all this have to do with the blues? Well, when we ask ourselves what it was that African American music brought to this nation that was so hungrily devoured, we need to examine the state of the American soul, what it needed to regain its health, and whether this quality can be found in the blues. The point is that we are a culture literally imprisoned in our own minds. We think we experience reality, but when most of us are cut off from our own bodies and feelings to varying degrees, what we experience must be incomplete. The more we merge with technology, the less life we feel. This loss of touch with our bodily life has been creeping into our culture for a good century and a half (since the start of the industrial revolution), with the last fifty years bringing particularly disorienting and powerful changes to our lives.

Not even music has escaped the effects of this technological curse: electronic rhythms and computer-sampled sounds are beginning to dominate the airwaves. Alan Lomax says that ". . .the sound that is being voiced on the world is rather empty and sometimes extremely unpleasant, maybe even dangerous. When you make rhythm with a machine, it loses its real human vitality"[13] This kind of music is the very antithesis of the blues. When the Yardbirds played with Sonny Boy Williamson in the sixties, he ". . . told them that his idea for tempo was looking at how animals or people walk, relating the physical movement to the feel of the tempo in the music."[14] But these days, music is drifting further and further away from its roots in the physical world, and the result is a product that has little or nothing to do with real human concerns or any kind of real feeling. There is a palpable difference between music made by a machine and that created by a human being.

At first, Americans seemed willing to embrace the idea of a new technocratic utopia. But, by the mid-fifties and early sixties, restlessness was beginning to surface, as the youth began looking for something more real. When the technocratic society became too stultifying for young people—who were still vibrant, full of energy and creativity—they turned to whatever antidote they could find. They did not want to succumb to this slavery to technology—the body's urge to celebrate, to feel, would not be suppressed. The creature that was sleeping under this veneer of repression and silence was beginning to stir. There was a tremendous current of unvoiced sentiments in the air—raw pent-up feelings, sexual urges, longing, rage and pain—and it didn't come out in a clear linear way. The long-withheld communication was necessarily messy, loud, and involved the whole body's participation.

> Rock . . . has been necessary to break through the
> crust of self-consciousness accumulated over these
> last three thousand years. So that a place long asleep
> in us would wake . . . [In rock] there's no way to go
> but out of the culture and into the beat.
> —Michael Ventura[15]

The beat of the blues and rock and roll literally has the power to create a new culture. But it never would have happened without the first few brave pioneers who crossed race and class boundaries in order to bring the blues music they loved to a wider audience. Black music—jazz and rhythm and blues—was the only acceptable doorway white America had to an otherwise alien culture. Many musicians heard the beat of black music all around them, and their adaptations of it quickly garnered a larger audience.

Michael Bloomfield was one youth who would step out of his known universe and into the midst of this fascinating, still-forming, urban black culture. In the fifties, when he was growing up in a middle-class section of Chicago, he listened to the blues on the radio all the time. One day it dawned on him that this music was literally happening all around him; soon he and his friends were venturing into the ghettoes of Chicago with an unstoppable determination to learn from their idols. Michael would just walk up onstage, plug in his guitar and start jamming. He and his friends got beaten up several times (never by musicians), but he did manage to sit in with all the greats of Chicago blues—Muddy Waters, Buddy Guy, Junior Wells, Howlin' Wolf—and many of these blues legends took him under their wing. He desperately needed something from their world, and he didn't hesitate to get it. Bloomfield ended up not simply learning a genre of music, but being initiated into a new way of understanding and communicating with himself and others:

> When you played something, it was a lexicon, it was a language you had to learn. And when you could play in that language, the feedback you got then was of a very subtle nature. If you played the right note at the right time, there was a whole world of nuance that was understood . . . Somebody would yell at you "Play it!" or "Get down!" or whatever . . . there was a whole pattern of call and response . . . They didn't applaud; they could follow you note for note and know exactly when you were playing right from the heart, and they'd give that heart right back to you.[16]

Many whites approached this world with a kind of wistful devotion. For some, the attraction was the raw unrestrained eroticism that oozed out of the all-night blues clubs. For others it was the music itself, wild and free, like the heart's spontaneous movement to capture its destiny, to milk each moment for every last drop of passion.

Something like a religious fervor would grip these performers, and the crowd would respond in kind. Jack Kerouac described this longing as early as 1949, in *On the Road*:

> At lilac evening I walked with every muscle aching among the lights of 27th and Welton in the Denver coloured section, wishing I were a Negro, feeling that the best the white world had offered was not enough ecstasy for me, not enough life, joy, kicks, darkness, music, not enough night. I wished I were a Denver Mexican, or even a poor overworked Jap, anything but what I so Drearily was, a "white man" disillusioned.[17]

The beat poets were some of the only writers of that time to document this gnawing emptiness in the dark bowels of America and also to articulate the gift that African American music brought to this fragmented and lost culture— namely, a spark of pure untrammeled, brilliant life-energy in the midst of an ever more rigid and regimented society. The blues were leading them into

> . . . the secret world of voodoo, eroticism, crime and god-knows-what-else . . . one glimpses an unknown America with an imagination and imagery all its own. The blues poet has been where we are all afraid to go, as if there was a physical place, a forbidden place that corresponds to a place in ourselves where we experience the tragic sense of life and all its wonders. In that dive, in that all-night blues and soul club, we feel the full weight of our fate, we taste the nothingness at the heart of our being, we are simultaneously wretched and happy, we spit on it all, we

want to weep and raise hell, because the blues, in the end, is about a sadness older than the world, and there's no cure for that.

—Charles Simic[18]

In contemporary culture there is no reference point whatsoever for this kind of journey into hell. We grew up believing that this "forbidden place" should be avoided at all costs, and that those who actually went into this "dark night of the soul" *willingly* had to be dangerous or even insane. There is no way to explain this attraction to taste the nothingness at the heart of our being to those who have not experienced it. One day we simply realize that that's what we need to do.

Letting ourselves be thoroughly defeated by life is actually a road to a kind of transcendence, and for our times it may be *the* road. That's why the blues has been so embraced by ordinary people around the world. The transcendence of allowing defeat is the relief that comes with the surrender of hope, with dropping the burden of all our schemes and expectations about making life better. I like to think that one day I'm going to finally win the jackpot or be carried away by angels. But when I realize that no one can win the game of life, many doors open up, although they may not be the ones I was expecting. I may never get the respect I was looking for, or whatever it was I craved to make me feel whole. But then I realize that wholeness comes from getting bigger than who I thought I was.

Rockin' Our Blues Away

Now mama used to say — rock and roll always rule
My mama used to say — that rock and roll gonna rule
But this little baby — she gone to the hard blues school
(That sweet blues school)

—Shri, *Blues School*[19]

In the 1940s and '50s, when white America ventured across the tracks and found the blues, they found that the music corresponded to the blues that they felt in their own souls. Yet, as entranced and seduced as they were by the music, American culture as a whole couldn't fully embody what it took to live the blues. Rock and roll was the inevitable compromise: a Janus-faced genre that for generations has alternated between living the kind of raw, naked passion that characterizes the blues, and jettisoning real feeling for the sake of money and popularity.

> Rock and roll is a means of escape from reality. We write the lyrics deliberately vague. The songs aren't addressed to anybody real, but to dream characters. The songs are egocentric and dreamy. Lots of basic blues ideas wouldn't wash as rock and roll because the blues are too real, too earthy. . .You're rarely going to hear even a plain happy rock and roll song, because happiness is a real emotion.
>
> —Jerry Leiber, co-writer of the song
> *Hound Dog*[20]

When songwriting becomes geared toward commercial success rather than the spontaneous expression of being, it loses its ability to touch people in a real way. Almost immediately following Elvis' meteoric rise to stardom, the forces of popular culture began saccharinizing the music. The beat of the blues was straightened out so that white hips could sway to it. The "blue" notes that didn't fit into the white scale system-the slides, bends, and quavers of voice, guitar or harmonica-were adapted to the sensibilities of white ears and white vocal cords. Above all, the lyrics were infused with enough sweetener to withstand the stern and watchful eyes of the moralists. That meant the lyrics had to sink to the level of the average teeny-bopper while simultaneously not offending their parents.

Those who fought the intrusion of black music into white society blamed its free and outspoken attitude about sex. But there were other urgent needs that the blues addressed besides sex, and I believe that these were just as threatening. Ecstasy, love, longing, desire, heartbreak, loneliness, despair—the blues charts the whole terrain of the human heart, from the starry heights to the bitter depths; but the real troubles of the blues were too much for pop culture. The hits of the day were also full of love songs—teenage laments about pining, first losses and breakups; but the range of emotion was more narrow. Hot sexual passion, rage-filled revenge, inconsolable heartbreak—intense, uncontrollable feelings such as these were forbidden territory.

The law of popular music is to constantly charm and delight people so that they keep buying records; it avoids shaking people up too much, or depressing them, or reminding them of their darkest passions and most difficult conflicts. If you want to sell records, whatever you do, don't remind anyone of their essential aloneness, or the inevitability of suffering in this life. To keep the people buying it's necessary to treat them gently, even coddle them with illusion. So the real blues is a hard sell, because it can't compete with the whole range of products designed to make us feel immediately happy with no effort. Soul and consumerism are like oil and water—they just don't mix.

The blues is about real things that happen to real people. It can't be glamorized. With the blues, we're not trying to escape our reality at all: we want to make it more vivid, more alive. In the beginning, blues artists weren't trying to sell millions of records; they were simply expressing what was in their hearts. Even the greatest blues performers never reach the unearthly heights that some rock and roll performers have reached because the blues is more down to earth. Also, I don't think the genre itself allows for that kind of god-like, superstar stature. Blues came out of a world for which the height of achievement was to be treated with the kindness and respect due any human being. If a blues artist rose out of obscurity to star stature, gratitude and a desire to help others was the most common response. The blues has to remain humble, or it's just not the blues.

Rock and roll borrowed a lot of things from the blues, but it missed a few too. One of the biggest traps for many rockers was glamour and vanity, which rob the music of its soul. In all the excitement and fervor of those wild, early rock and roll days, many were all too ready to jump into the musical experiment and move their bodies in ways never before imagined. In all this heady intoxication it was easy to overlook that this music originated in an intense cauldron of raw feeling: the black South.

For generations African Americans had demonstrated that they were profoundly in touch with their bodies in a way that simultaneously shocked and attracted white America. By far, music was the predominant means for whites to interface with this almost alien culture. More than anything, music helped bring us together (and we still have a *long* way to go). Appropriating black music was an acceptable way to learn about and appreciate black culture, because it still supported white hegemony: The blacks did the heavy work of creating a broad and unique musical culture, and the whites reaped the harvest, repackaged and sold it as rock and roll, and profited royally, while great black artists continued playing local clubs and eking out a living.

In fact, even as America was busy mining the soul of black culture, we took pains to hide what was really going on. How could we admit it? The most powerful, free and progressive nation on earth, turning to the common people, the lowest rung on the societal ladder, for wisdom and healing? Here was the last great theft of African culture. After generations of profiting from their arduous physical labor, we needed something more, something we had lost in ourselves along the way.

We drank from this well of juicy passion and life lived from the heart, but we did not dare to drink it to the dregs. The sexual and emotional freedom of black music seduced us, but Americans were not interested in serious relationship, for then we would learn the awful truth behind the blues, that it was an outlet for an entire culture that had been mercilessly abused. We thought we could take the part of the message that we liked and ignore what we didn't want to deal with. But really it is impossible to understand the blues without knowing where they come from, because then we are only appreciating them for what we think they are, not for what they're actually expressing. The beautiful grace, sweet soul and erotic abandon of the blues can only be fully appreciated against the backdrop of the profound pain and misery many endured. Otherwise we trivialize what the blues is: a profound affirmation of life and the inherent dignity of humanity in the face of demeaning and heartbreaking circumstances.

The Wages of Comfort

It is all too easy to lose sight of the real message of this music when we are surrounded by comfort—I am certainly no exception. One night we were playing the Tiffany Tree Lounge, a ritzy restaurant with twenty-five-dollar entrees. We were told to haul our equipment in "nonchalantly" so as not to disturb the atmosphere of fine dining. A life-size replica of a tree with multi-colored glass leaves "grew" from behind the bar and draped its patrons in opulent ambiance. The place was smoke-free and juke-box-free, so sedate it was almost eerie. Sitting there in our plush chairs, we wondered if anyone here even gave a damn about the blues.

As always, we had no choice but to play on through it all, and despite our reservations we had a pretty good first set. The crowd wasn't going anywhere and they were paying attention, but they did not seem to be deeply moved. Then Lee came up to finish off the set with several traditional blues songs. He enjoys bantering with the crowd, and saying whatever happens to be passing through his mind at the time.

"That was called *My Bleeding Heart*. Well, all most people ever get to in their lives is a bleeding mind. A bleeding heart wouldn't be so bad—at least you get to *feel*."

"Oh God," I thought, "is Lee going to scare these people away." It felt a little too real for the Tiffany Tree Lounge.

Lee continued, a hint of tenderness in his voice: "I apologize if I'm saying anything that doesn't exactly resonate. Most of the places that we play in are not so comfortable—most of the people there are pretty wounded. Most of you look pretty well off. You're damn lucky."

A well-dressed but evidently lonely patron at the bar who had been listening to us all night chimed in: "You got the 'off' part right."

Lee, snickering: "There's a man after my own heart."

Lee's comments sent me reeling, and I jumped into the next song before anything else could be said. It was *Smokestack Lightning*, with its words full of dark eroticism and Delta mystery, riding a timeless guitar riff into the endless night. Lee was lost in the song, utterly abandoned to the story he was telling, his whole body singing. For him, the words, the rhythm, the whole musical package is merely a vehicle to communicate raw presence. The music became utterly alive—immersing myself in the song, my mind's chatter faded away, allowing the deeper impulses of my body to speak. Allowed to relax into its natural state, the body simply plays.

As I looked about the room, I could see that Lee had taken a few passengers on his strange voyage; his honest appraisal of the situation had captured the otherwise apathetic crowd. The lonely man at the bar was spellbound, enthralled by Lee's urgency and conviction. I felt a little ashamed at my own embarrassment. It was not the audience who couldn't take it—it was myself, too worried about what people will think. I was reminded once again that the real blues is not about making people momentarily happy—it's about telling the truth. And when I saw the enraptured faces of the bar patrons I realized that as much as we want to be entertained, we want the truth even more—ultimately, the truth can make us happier.

Chapter 7

The Heart of the Blues

The reason people make lyric poems and blues songs is because our life is short, sweet, and fleeting. The blues bear witness to the strangeness of each individual's fate. It begins wordlessly in a moan, a stamp of the foot, a sigh, a hum, and then seeks words for that something or other that has no name in any language and for which all poetry and music seeks an approximation.

—Charles Simic[1]

Western culture badly needs a religion of the underbelly of life, a religion rising up from the shacks and tenements, the nightclubs and dance halls, the streetcorner bazaars where sex sells and pills save. Instead of floating down from on high to preach a refined moral vision, the blues-people preach the nitty-gritty details of their lives, just as their ancestors did in Africa, where religion and music accompanied a person's smallest acts, bringing the spirit down to earth, where we humans obviously belong.

As the chronicler of the shifting moods of the human heart, blues music tells our story like nothing else can. In our complex world obsessed with facts and data, the blues stands for simpler, more profound truths: the distillation of life felt through the body, the inevitability of suffering, a resolute faith in ordinary life, and the ineluctable hunger of love. Life becomes much simpler when we can break it down to its bare essentials.

Unfortunately, as I listen to the endless cultural debates that fil-
ter into my private world through the miracle of radio waves, I find
that instead of taking this invitation to simplify, we as a people are
building life up into more and more complexity, and thus drowning
in a sea of trivia. What a relief it would be if the talk show host
asked people to call in and just speak about their loneliness: how it
crept up on them unexpectedly; how it accompanied them everywhere like an invisible friend; or how it often assaulted them in the
midst of social occasions.

> That's the way a lot of people is today: they got
> the blues and don't know it.
>
> —Big Bill Broonzy

Americans are like a "lonely crowd," as a famous sociological
study of the 1950s put it. A lot of exciting and important activity
seems to be happening on the surface, but underneath all the dis-
tractions there is actually less and less human contact taking place.

The 1900s has been a tumultuous century that has seen two
world wars, ecological disasters, intractable poverty, massive increas-
es in drug addiction, and a new wave of ultra-violent crime and ter-
rorism. Cultural moorings have become unglued; the old, comforting
philosophies no longer assuage our fears. No wonder this has been
called the Age of Anxiety: we don't even know who we are anymore.
On a lonely planet in the middle of a vast mysterious galaxy, we are
poised to wreak ecological or military destruction on a scale that is
unthinkable. For a country with as much political freedom, education
and material comfort as any in the world, we are a profoundly dis-
satisfied bunch. Most of us are too busy seeking comfort to wonder
or worry about the nagging feeling that there is a hole at the center

of our grandest schemes and projects; we think we're really in control, but this belies our paralyzing fear that maybe we're not. Ultimately, the blues is a journey into the void—a void that has taken up residence at the core of contemporary culture.

One way to describe the malaise that is gripping Western society is *soul loss*, i.e., losing touch with the primal forces that inform and move us—sex, love, passion, creativity, the cycles of nature, death.

The experience of *soul* brings meaning to our lives; it opens us up to the primordial mystery of existence. While "soul" can't be defined, we can all feel it. For instance, we know when a performer has soul, and when he or she is just going through the motions. We often say that a soulful performance "inspires us," "touches our heart," or even that it "sets us on fire." We also know when work that we do "feeds our soul," rather than simply providing a means of making a living. We know when a man or woman has that extra spark that captures our romantic interest. Maybe we can't pin down this elusive quality of soul, but we certainly recognize it—this essence that lives in and breathes divine presence.

Blacks have traditionally referred to their musical expressions as "soul music," and this should not be taken lightly. True, often the titles that get bandied about make us grin: "James Brown, The Godfather of Soul," "Thelonious Monk, High Priest of Bop." But these descriptions are not meant to be humorous; they point to the pervasive presence of spirituality in all genres of black music, which has the crucial function of keeping alive individual souls as well as the collective soul of the community. Musical performance and participation in the black community are vital spiritual acts whose roots reach down into the soil of the African continent, where the collective history of all the peoples of the earth finds a common ancestry.

Soul has always been invoked by music, and African music has always been about soul. Blues songs are about all sorts of things, but this common message of soul survival underlies them all. It is encoded in the dense layers of rhythm that are so crucial to almost all black music, and it tells its story regardless of the words that are being sung.

Everyone has the seed of soul, but it doesn't grow at the same rate for each person. Soul is accumulated through life experience, especially hardship and suffering. When life seems to provide no options, we are forced to search inside ourselves for a strength of being that is untouched by the vicissitudes of circumstance. This explains why outcast groups are able to create music that is dripping with soul, because they have earned it through difficult and painful life experience. The blues has served this function of helping people journey through the inevitable struggles of becoming human, leading them to a deeper understanding of themselves and their lives. It is one man or woman's testament of anguish, remorse, acceptance and joy.

You Get to Church Now, Ya Hear!

The testament of human agony and ecstasy doesn't arise in a vacuum; it is sanctified in the Church of the Blues, in the local bars and juke joints, at festivals and concert halls and even on streetcorners, wherever crowds of believers come to dance and drink and revel in that "old-time feeling." The Church of the Blues is never a respectable, clean, quiet place for self-reflection. It is a hot, dark, sweaty cauldron of desire and despair, loneliness and hope. When one enters a "respectable" church one expects to feel transported out of his or her ordinary self into a nobler, more righteous state. When one enters the blues church however, one sinks down into the swamp of their humanity. The weathered sign over the door proclaims, "Sinners welcome."

As you enter the blues club—the all-night altar of funk—the

smoky incense haze seeps into your lungs. You push past the throngs of people to the bar and order a drink to put yourself "in the mood." There is an air of expectancy as the band putters around the stage, tuning up, joking, surveying the whole array of seekers for the blues truth. The singer/preacher is a woman, elegantly dressed, gray hairs starting to tell their story, her plump and vibrant body moving with grace and confidence. Her face radiates soft vulnerability, able to produce a range of expression from smiles of compassion to tears of despair. She beckons you with an undeniable presence of one who has journeyed to many places inside herself—maybe she wants to let you in on a few secrets!

You've been following a twinge of longing that has no name, a desire to tap into a life as yet not wholly lived. No, you probably wouldn't say these things if asked why you came to this local blues club tonight. But an honest appraisal of the scene will reveal a startling truth: that many people are here for an experience beyond mere entertainment; for them, the blues is a kind of church. How else can we explain their sometimes overjoyed, heartfelt gratitude for the music? They come looking for a key to their souls, to return to a state of lost innocence. This night is not unlike the communal rituals of our ancestors, who have passed down their timeless knowledge of "the boogie."

Ultimately, with the blues you know that it's allright, and that we're all in this together. Many people accuse the blues of being downhearted and depressing, but those who play the music and those who are devoted listeners approach it for exactly the opposite reason: because it lifts their spirits. The blues *is* a sad music—it mourns the loss of love—but that is different than being depressing. Sadness is actually a life-positive emotion because it acknowledges the power of love, while depression asserts that it never existed to begin with. The blues is not only about pain and suffering; really it is about celebration in the midst of pain and suffering. The blues coaxes and cajoles us to accept our sorrow and despair *and* our joy and ecstasy. One thing is for sure: we need wide arms to embrace it all. No, there is no repair in the church of the blues, no salvation, no heaven. The real miracle in this church is the perfect acceptance of ordinary life. The Heart of God beats in this world, the world right under our feet, the world inside our breast.

Love in Hell

> *People cannot love physically and spiritually (the two cannot be separated!) until they have been up against the edge of life, experiencing the hurt and pain of existence. They cannot appreciate the feel and touch of life nor express the beauty of giving themselves to each other in community, in love, and in sex until they know the brokenness of existence . . .*
>
> —Stephen Cone[2]

A case could be made that the emergence of the blues in our society was a major factor in leading the way toward the sexual revolution, because the music preached the salvific nature of love and sex. Yet, a real sexual revolution has nothing to do with sleeping with whomever we want, whenever we want; it can only come about by an inner revolution, by allowing the energy of our sexuality to infiltrate our heart—then our love becomes fiery and passionate while our lust becomes sweet and tender. A mature lover, as the quote by Cone suggests, stops protecting himself and allows his woundedness to permeate his life. Basically, Cone is saying that we can't love until we acknowledge our broken heart. That is the message in the blues that can *really* lead us to a revolution in our sexual relationships.

There is so much shame, confusion and denial around love and sex in this culture that we could go our whole lives floating in the waters of our unfulfilled desires, constantly tossed about by the waves of our passions, getting nowhere. It takes courage to let go and sink to the bottom, to be honest about how it really is for us. For me, it is liberating (and scary) to allow all the emotional detritus that has built up around women to move and express itself. Playing the blues is the perfect vehicle for this expression, because it lets me look at sex directly, in a cleaner way. My rage, loneliness, blind lust, shame, longing—all gets to hang out. In the following quote, Lawrence Levine sums up why this music is so refreshing when it comes to matters of love:

> The blues [are] far less pervaded by self-pity, the profound fatalism, and the very real disillusionment that marked American popular music. [Their] strong sense of humor and proportion . . . prevent[s] even the most pitiable lover from posturing. [In the blues] love seldom resembled the ethereal, ideal relationship so often pictured in popular songs. Love was depicted as a fragile, often ambivalent relationship between imperfect beings.[3]

The blues are a primer on how to win and lose the game of love. "No form of music yet evolved has been able to express so simply and directly the frustrations, satisfactions, and reversals of the mating game."[4] The lessons are simple; at least all the wrong moves are spelled out clearly.

Witness the great blues guitarists strutting their stuff, or those powerful blues mamas singing their hearts out. What tremendous power is available in freeing it all up, allowing ourselves to be, accepting life! It's what makes us juicy. But when we refuse to or are not able to accept ourselves, we are bound to continue making the same old mistakes. Those mistakes are the subject of ninety percent of all blues songs.

Most of us are in conflict over love. Often, when we look inside ourselves we find a full-scale war. On one side is our desire for union, which includes relationship, intimacy, love and sex. This position can make us act rashly, without thinking—sometimes that's good, sometimes not. This powerful drive encompasses physical, emotional and spiritual dimensions; ultimately, it is the recognition that we need relationship to keep our emotional heart beating.

The other position in the battle is the terror of losing ourselves in love. Many fears come up around falling in love: fear of getting hurt or abandoned; fear of being responsible and committed to someone; fear of loss of control. But the deepest fear is that of losing ourselves, not knowing where we end and where someone else begins, for the more we truly love, the more we disappear. The phrase "falling in love" conjures a threatening image. Love is death, the demise of our sense that we are separate beings. The death that love offers can be either blissful or terrifying.

Because it engenders our deepest desires and fears, love is the greatest, most common theme in art throughout the world. It fills the songbooks of all the world's music, and it totally dominates the blues. Pop music everywhere is devoted to the subject of love. That's why Willie Dixon could recognize the blues in Middle-Eastern music, because longing has its own language, beyond words. We hear love in flamenco, Gregorian chant, Sufi whirling-dervish music, to name just a few forms. And not only is love sung about everywhere, but it has dozens of different moods or flavors. Love is so vast that we can sing about it in a hundred ways and still call it love.

This source of our greatest ecstasy also seems to be the taproot of our most bitter suffering. We are filled with paradoxes and contradictions concerning love. We've all probably heard the saying: "Women: can't live with them; can't live without them." Maybe women say something similar about men. But we could all say the same thing about love itself, so in that sense it is the great equalizer between the sexes. Love can be the key to our freedom and happiness one day and turn into an excruciating burden overnight. What is this mercurial substance that plays with our moods as if we were puppets? We feel helpless in its grasp, as suddenly all control slips through our fingers.

Our lyricist, Lee Lozowick, poignantly sums up the dilemmas of relationship between the sexes:

> One thing 'bout men and women
> that surely is the same
> both can have a broken heart
> oh ain't it a shame
> this can bring us together
> or tear us wide apart
> it's the great equalizer
> right from the start
>
> The battle of the sexes
> don't seem like its worth the price
> the posing and the vanities
> and all the bad advice
> we both shed the same warm tears
> we feel the same pain
> and the aching emptiness
> still pounds in both our brain

What were we once thinking
when we began this fight
Did we guess the consequences
would be such lonely nights
What was it got into us
to make us reject love
It's the great equalizer
when push comes to shove

One thing 'bout men and women
that is the bottom line
We don't want to be alone
even though we say we're fine
We each want one another
so why need this war
It's the great equalizer
no one gets a score
—*The Great Equalizer*[5]

Blues singers say that love is a force that overpowers our individual wills, and many great philosophers and religions agree with that statement. Love cannot be argued with, bargained with, bought or sold. It comes boldly of its own accord and sometimes leaves in the same manner. Love simply is—it reigns supreme in this world, and the blues singer knows that it will always triumph in the end. Poetry and music were invented just so that human beings could have a way to describe love. That is really the only function of art.

Playing for the People

When Shri started out, we straddled the fence between playing blues and rock and could have gone either way. One attraction to the blues was that the club owners in the blues world were usually straightforward, down-to-earth people who were genuinely interested in the music, while rock club owners did not seem to be as interested in the music as they were in making a buck. The audiences at blues clubs also seemed to come more for the music than anything else. Although we were raised on rock and roll, we soon began to feel that our hearts were in the blues—it satisfied deep appetites within all of us. And playing the blues was really taking part in a tradition, which involved a lot of integrity in staying true to the music. Altogether, the blues is a more challenging genre, but it has been a more rewarding one as well.

At some of the larger venues we have played, the kind of intimacy with the audience that the blues requires is sometimes hard to come by. A friend we met at the Peer R & B Festival in Belgium, James from the St. Gabriel's Celestial Brass Band, was sincerely hurt by the lack of relationship between audience and performers that the music industry encouraged. He entreated us to not get hooked by an attitude of exclusivity:

> There are people here that really need to get backstage, but they aren't allowed. It's a shame. Don't ever forget who you're playing for. Man, there are musicians who are totally cut off from the people. I mean, why can't I go up and talk to Mick Jagger. Why not? 'Cause the record company won't allow it. Don't forget the people—that's what it's all about.

James couldn't understand how the artist could become cut off from his or her audience. Like man and woman, rain and sunshine, joy and pain, the interdependence of band and audience was totally

175

obvious to him. He lives in a world where music is a community event, and serves a vital function. For James and for us, a true band is not about a bunch of separate egos getting their hit of musical bliss. It's about a group of people coming together in understanding and celebration. Our job is not about making people admire us, it's about making people happy.

Many of the men in the St. Gabriel's Band complained bitterly about the general apathy and lack of musical appreciation they found in America, and they were unanimous in voting the European audiences more attentive and responsive. In short, the Europeans cared about the music. But as James and the other musicians talked further, they reserved their harshest criticism for the music industry, which they blamed for separating the artist and the audience. High ticket prices were driving away the poor people, "the people who really need this music." Those who need a healing ceremony to release them from their daily drudgery are the very ones who often can't afford it.

The blues tells everyone's story, a story told not so much through facts as through feeling. We play in order to bring life to an almost unbearably simple, crystal clear point of longing, burning deep into the soul, inescapable. We cease being human when we stop longing, when we cease to strive for something higher, or more passionate, or more meaningful. It seems that's why human beings showed up on this planet, to be the ones who cry out to heaven.

Longing is the heart's cry and the heart's answer, the pain of limitation and aloneness, and the tender joy of intimacy. It is present at birth, in death, in first kisses and in final partings. It is present in everything we try to achieve or build. It was there when Columbus sailed for the New World, as Mother Teresa cared for dying lepers, when Michaelangelo sculpted David, when Einstein postulated the theory of relativity, and on and on. But longing is not only a path for visionaries; it is the path of the everyday person and is present in our smallest acts of gratitude, kindness and love. We cannot escape it; we may divert or pervert it, but we can never shut it off.

The message of the blues that Shri sings is that this longing is what makes us human, and it is *never* going away. This is a far cry from the messages with which our culture barrages us night and day. Consumer society doesn't work if people really know they have the blues, because all advertising is based on the premise that the next purchase is going to make it all better. But if you know you have the blues, really know it, then you know that no purchase, no new relationship, no self-help plan, in fact *nothing* outside of yourself is going to make it all better.

Often, we don't see that what we really want is simply to be happy, not to *have* anything in particular. We are just incredibly mixed up on *how* to be happy. Yet, look at children: without power, possessions or a list of goals to achieve, they have the ability to know happiness as a full-body experience, and they communicate this easily to anyone around them who is the least bit open. Only the most damaged individuals are unable to see the joy and innocence that an infant carries into the world. I believe it is that state of the innocent child that people are longing for, a state of internal confidence that, despite all the heartache and frustration of human life, the world is inherently good, that we can rest in a state of love, free from all the considerations, fears and narrow-mindedness with which we are chronically plagued. Unfortunately, in the process of growing up, learning how to do all the complex things we have to do and all the ways we have to be to get along in this society, we slowly forget this simple knowledge and replace it with a super-imposed self that we need if we are to function in this world.

I think we can reclaim our lost innocence. For instance, in the blues, if we feel it, if it happened to us, we can sing it out, loud! Innocence is above all a state free from crippling shame: no feeling or experience is barred from expression. Blues addresses the peculiarly American, or at least Western, ailment—lack of feeling and enthusiasm for life. (The French call it *joie de vivre*.) The problem is not so much with *what* people are feeling as with the fact that they aren't feeling, period. The old saying goes, "Blues is a feeling." If I could dare to improve on it I would say, "Blues *is* feeling." It doesn't matter what we are feeling, we just need to get down into it. And from the feeling comes the healing, the salvation and the grace. The blues is the religion of the streets.

Shri plays the blues because this music holds the promise of reconnecting us and our audiences with our heart's desire. Maybe we have turned away from it all our lives because our secret joys and dreams were thwarted at an early age. Maybe we became disillusioned, the peculiar malady of modern life. Maybe we did not want to feel the pain of being refused our birthright, of the world saying, "No!" to our basically good humanity. Yet, sooner or later, we found out that it was even more deeply dissatisfying to give up—we found we were refusing ourselves without anyone's help.

Earlier this century the blues was a healing balm for the pain of black men and women imprisoned in a world of poverty and brutality. Today it speaks to all of us. Trapped in a life-negating world of our own making, mocked by celluloid ghosts, digital demons and metal monoliths, there is a palpable yearning in many societies for a richer, more meaningful way of life. We can never know the depths of suffering that forged African American music: tragedy on a scale unimaginable for most of us. Nevertheless, our own experience, our own journey into our humanity *is* real for us—it can take us to the heart of the blues, which, like any authentic art form, strikes a universal chord. To search for that chord is not only to find what is real in the blues; it is to search within ourselves for the shared feelings that make humanity one body.

The Arizona Café in Brest, France

In 1996, our tour of France brought us into the heart of Bretagne, the northwest corner of France where an ancient Celtic culture still thrives. As we approached the port city of Brest in our Renault mini-van, the road signs began to appear in both French and Gaelic—now we felt like we were in a doubly strange land. But it didn't matter because the salty wind blowing in over the rolling green hills from the sea felt invigorating. We were excited because we had all grown up near the ocean on the east coast of the U.S.; but now, living in the middle of the Arizona desert, and most of us having hardly seen the ocean in years, the deep green hills of Bretagne were a soothing relief from the dusty roads we usually travel back home.

The town of Brest was lively but a little seedy, what you would expect from a seaport. We all thought it was auspicious that we were playing a club named after our home state. The place was filled with western arcana of all kinds: posters of cowboys and Indians riding past majestic mesas; leather saddles; a long classic wooden bar; and, of course, animal skulls. Taken out of their common habitat, those white shining skulls somehow took on the aura of ritual objects, creating an ominous and foreboding presence as they peered down at me. As if that wasn't enough, as we pulled up behind the bar to unload our equipment, we noticed that there was an old cemetery just over a dilapidated stone wall. For some reason, the phrase "hellhounds on my trail" (the title of a Robert Johnson song) popped into my mind. I had a feeling these were going to be a powerful couple of nights.

We were scheduled to play from 11:30 P.M. till 3:30 A.M., by far the latest we had ever been asked to play (usually in the States we stop by one o'clock). The bar was packed when we kicked into our set, and unbelievably it got more and more crowded as the night wore on. This was not the France we were used to! The whole scene

179

reminded me of pubs I had been to in Ireland, which were more like social clubs where everyone knew each other, rather than bars where a bunch of strangers try to pick up a companion for the night. The people were more wild and carefree, more "in your face" than we had ever seen. Even biker bars back home didn't compare to the raw energy that was present that night. The crowd seemed to be consciously provoking us to play over the top, to let go and get wild, pushing us to the peak of our skills and beyond. Shukyo was attacking her drum set with unbelievable force; they seemed to shrink down to the size of toys next to her radiant brightness. Tina and I were bouncing around the stage playfully, while Deborah's voice, raw and passionate in its urgency, ripped through the room, jolting people into recognition of something more real than the glass of beer sitting in front of them. In moments like these, trying to hold the band together becomes more like riding a bucking bronco, as we all try to create music out of this almost violently uncontrollable energy.

People were screaming and laughing and banging on tables. The owner of the bar had a brass bell that he began to ring about half way through the first set, and by the end he was frantically ringing it after each song, and yelling out something in French which sounded pretty good. At 3:30 we were supposed to end, but came back for an encore with *Blind Devotion*. They loved it and proceeded to pound on the walls, floors and tables in unison while the owner rang his bell with one hand and pounded on the wall with the other until we agreed to do another song. We ended with *You Can Have My Husband* and then we unplugged the microphone and ran out the back door so that we'd be able to stop and finally get back to our hotel.

It was probably our highest moment together onstage since we started playing three years earlier. We went back to our hotel in a mood of tremendous appreciation of what our work together could create. That night we all experienced a freedom onstage that was exhilarating, the kind of wild abandon we all play for. Yet, even as we reveled in the glorious afterglow of musical bliss, the raw sensuousness that had been unleashed within all of us was a bit frightening. The next day we woke up around noon, slightly dazed, as if we had just been on another planet the night before. Now we were supposed to go sightseeing around Brest and pretend everything was normal?!? I could feel an edge of anxiety enter the group, as the previous night had brought us all uncomfortably close. I chose to spend the day alone; the feeling of intimacy the previous night was a little too real for me, and I didn't know how much of it I could take.

So, later that night, it was understandable when our second show at the Arizona Café began tentatively. We all knew the door of possibility was still open, but we were ignoring it, pretending it didn't exist, even as an unbearable yearning to reach those heights once again ached within us. It felt like something had to give; we were just biding time, waiting for the signal. For the right mood to strike, we are dependent on many factors beyond our control: the receptivity of the audience, the mood of everyone in the band, the ambiance of the club, maybe even the position of the stars. The approach is something like prayer, asking for the gift that the music can offer, knowing that we cannot produce it on our own. Who knows what elements are needed to create inspiration? The Muse comes and goes of her own accord on wings of whimsy.

This time the moment of breakthrough came when another musician we had met walked into the club. He was a small but wiry French man, barely twenty, with a little whip of blond hair and an air of irrepressible mischief (at our gig the night before he had helped to incite the crowd to near hysteria). He reminded me of the god Pan, with his bawdy, sexually suggestive ways and his sneer of contempt for uptight convention. He came over toward the stage, beer in hand, toasting us, yelling out something unintelligible in a local

French dialect. When I saw the glint of craziness in his eyes, something in me broke. Faltering musical foreplay gave way to primitive abandon. We were taking off again—the club changed from a dim, smoky room to a bright and vibrant scene.

It was one of those nights when the whole room not only lit up—it was on fire! Deborah pushed herself energetically and creatively more than I had ever seen her, going beyond previous limits of fear. At times I worried if her voice would be okay for the next day's festival. Usually she protects her voice before important events—this night she was going for broke. The crowd went wild; there was barely enough free space to get through the room, but somehow everyone was dancing. Now Deborah was provoking them. It was a game to see who could get crazier, us or the audience. Everybody was winning.

Then the mood took a surprising shift. We came to a brand new song we had never performed before in public, *Earthly Love*. It's a slow jazzy ballad, not our standard repertoire. The atmosphere softened dramatically, as when children who were running wild one minute suddenly run out of energy and get very still and quietly attentive. Deborah's voice was like warm honey, plaintive, drawing in lost bees with a soothing message.

> Some people say
> that life can be hell
> but the flames can burn
> in sweet love just as well
> Take your love out of your pocket
> There's no need to be alone
> I want you to know
> I'll bring your fine love home

Don't be so fast to
seek heaven above
before you sink down
to that earthly love
come here babe
give your soul to me
I'll give you a drink
of ecstasy

It may often seem
that life is pretty tough
and without love, I'll tell ya
yes it gets pretty rough
But come here to me darlin'
I'll soothe your cares away
and I'll show you all the pleasures
that love holds every day
     —Shri, *Earthly Love*[6]

Deborah sang these sweet words with so much real compassion
and tenderness that people couldn't help but respond; she relin-
quished her wounded heart in order to bring a sense of healing and
relief to others, baring an innocence and vulnerability that was
almost miraculous, what everyone wants deep down but is too afraid
to really embrace. Her mission (and it is clear that she sees it like
this) is to keep pointing everyone toward real life, real joy, real pain,
real love. In her day-to-day life she is searching as much as anyone
else, but when she sings she's onto something, she's there, and everybody can feel it.

That night, Deborah was not just singing; her voice trembled on
the edge of prayer, threatening to slide into redemption and grace.

But this was not the kind of prayer many of us were taught—this was the heart's cry, naked and unadorned, as if she had been broken open by God's very own hand. In Deborah's blues there was no hidden agenda or subterfuge, no strategy or philosophy—it was simply this pain, this joy, this loneliness, this longing. What is prayer if not the spontaneous expression of the shifting moods of the heart? And what is a human being without the possibility of this expression? As Deborah sang I closed my eyes and listened to her voice, and found myself floating in a kind of reverie. The room became dark and liquid, alive, nurturing: like a womb, everything completely peaceful. I felt surrounded by a benevolent feminine presence and filled with an immense sense of gratitude and devotion. As I look back on that one moment, it was worth all the tension and frustration of our first tour of France.

After that magical set we stepped out back for some air. Just the four of us, standing between a bar and a graveyard, enjoying each other's company. I felt so relaxed, so complete. We walked together down the deserted foggy streets singing *You Got to Move*, a Fred McDowell spiritual, and other old blues songs that we barely knew the words to. For the first time since I had joined the band three years earlier, I did not feel any sense of separation between myself and the others. Previously, the fact of being the only man in the band had gnawed away at me, but now it meant nothing. I saw how much we all depend upon and support one another. Shri was a sanctuary where we could truly be ourselves.

The blues and all music of the heart is about rediscovering ourselves and our surroundings. Playing the blues repaints the world with an electric brush stroke that illuminates the innate spark of creation everywhere I look. When we can truly see with the rich sparkling clarity that spontaneously arises from intense participation in life, then we can know our rightful place in the scheme of things.

The Blues Alive

Humanity has less to lose by embracing the depths than by pretending to the heights.

—Erica Jong[7]

The blues are the theme music for our times, an arresting juxtaposition of moods: a mournful message veiled with ironic wit, served steaming hot on an unabashedly sexy beat. The infectious groove, pulsing with the insistence of raw sexuality, yet laying back on itself at the same time, demands a response. The words probe the caverns of the heart, reminding us of the seemingly eternal occurrence of lost love. Remorse or loneliness may be kindled, but the beat insists—dance on through it all! It carries us and our feelings into a dynamic space where things can shift and be transformed. The unending good-time beat and the plangent melodies of unfulfilled desire blend together, telling us that joy and suffering can never be separated. The blues never lets us forget our humanity.

We come back to the blues again and again for many reasons. We want to be ecstatically grateful for our lives, to uncover the radiant goodness of the world that we vaguely recall. We want to release the burden of hiding our shortcomings, broken dreams and broken relationships, our remorse for our "sins."

When the music starts, there's a subtle pull, a longing, a feeling that we can finally let go and fall into a place we've simultaneously been seeking and running from all our lives. Welcome to the paradox of the blues. . .

It's not that I believed in
every word that you said
It's just that I was blinded

by the life you had led
It's not that I got trapped
by your pretense and your lies
I saw it all quite clearly
but I got hooked by your eyes

Your body said I should stay away
but your eyes said, "Come on in."
Some say the soul is mirrored there
well, I guess it must have been
I thought it was such good fortune
that led me here to you
I never would have figured
on the hoops you put me through

I trusted you and where am I now
all alone, wonderin' how
I got hooked by your eyes
I trusted you and what did I get
A broken heart I could never forget
I got hooked by your eyes

I should have been ready baby
to be your circus clown
But it's not what you wanted
I could see as you put me down
I guess you figured that you had
the perfect little slave
But that's a role that didn't fit me
so I choose this fate

It's not that I believed in
every word that you said
It's just that I was blinded
by the life you had led
It's not that I got trapped
by your pretense and your lies
I saw it all quite clearly
but I got hooked by your eyes

I trusted you and where am I now
all alone, wonderin' how
I got hooked by your eyes
I trusted you and what did I get
A broken heart I could never forget
I got hooked by your eyes
—Shri, *Hooked by Your Eyes*[8]

For the members of Shri, stepping onstage can be a moment that approaches the sacred, as we are filled with awe at the mystery of music and the endless possibilities it creates. All it takes is one note: just one note can contain the whole story of life from birth to death and everything in between; it can become a looking glass onto the universe, from an angle which was hitherto unknown. One note can gather our energy so completely into the present moment that we discover our world as if for the first time. One note can be a cry of despair, of wrenching agony, or of orgasmic delight, radiating throughout the hall, shimmering in the air, changing, pulsating, trembling, seeming to get closer to some mysterious goal with every moment. And before it ever ends it already carries with it a sense of loss, because we know it will fade and die and never reach the heights it was looking for. One note is the heartache of being human, of yearning for the impossible: perfect, undying love.

ENDNOTES

Chapter I

1. Simic, Charles. "No Cure for the Blues," p. 135, in *Antaeus: On Music.* No. 71/72, Autumn, 1993. Ed. by Daniel Halpern.

2. Lomax, Alan. *The Land Where the Blues Began.* New York: Pantheon Books, 1993, p. ix.

3. "I Be's Troubled" by McKinley Morganfield (Muddy Waters). Used by permission.

4. Unpublished song lyric, quoted in Lomax, p. 5.

5. Unpublished song lyric, quoted in Lomax, p. 171.

6. Lozowick, Lee. Unpublished lyric.

7. Quoted in: Obrecht, Jas, Editor. *Blues Guitar: The Men Who Made the Music.* From the pages of *Guitar Player* magazine. San Francisco: GPI Books, 1990, p. 98.

8. Quoted in Neff, Robert and Anthony Connor. *Blues.* Boston: David R. Godine, Publisher, 1975, p. 5.

9. Cone, Stephen R. *The Spirituals and the Blues.* Maryknoll: Orbis Books, 1972, p. 123.

10. Quoted in Obrecht, p. 130.

11. Wright, Richard, from the foreword to: Oliver, Paul. *The Blues Fell This Morning: The Meaning of the Blues.* Cambridge: Cambridge University Press, 1990, p. xv.

12. Wright, Richard. *12 Million Black Voices: A Folk History of the Negro in the U.S.* New York: Viking, 1941, p. 128.

13. Cone, p. 112.

14. Cone, p. 105.

15. Lorca, Frederico Garcia, quoted in Quintana, Bertha B. and Lois Gray Floyd. *¡Qué Gitano! Gypsies of Southern Spain.* New York: Holt, Rinehart and Winston, Inc., 1972, p. 50.

16. Quoted in Oliver, Paul. *Conversations with the Blues.* London: Cassell, 1965, p. 25.

17. Shines, Johnny. quoted in Obrecht, p. 20.

18. Hooker, John Lee. Quoted in Neff, p. 1.

19. Boyd, Eddie. "Five Long Years." Used by permission.

20. Quoted in Shreiner, Claus, Editor. *Flamenco: Gypsy Dance and Music from Andalusia.* Portland: Amadeus Press, 1985, p. 22.

21. Simic, p. 135.

22. Jong, Erica. *The Devil at Large.* New York: Random House, 1993, p. 8.

23. Charters, Sam. Notes to *J.D. Short and Son House: The Blues of the Mississippi Delta.* Folkways Album FA 2647.

24. Ellison, Ralph. *Shadow and Act.* New York: Signet Books, 1964, p. 247.

25. Lomax, p. xiv.

26. Quoted in Lomax, p. 460.

27. Quoted in Mossel, Eric. "Everyday I have the blues." Blues World #8 May, 1966, p.13.

28. Shines, Johnny. quoted in Neff, pp. 5-6. Used by permission.

29. Cone, p. 59.

30. Lomax, Alan. Quoted in an interview with Arnold Rypens, in *Back to the Roots,* #14 May, 1997, p. 33.

31. Quoted in: Stewart, Ollie. "What Price Jazz?" *The Chicago Defender*, April 7, 1934, p. 12.

32. Baraka, Amiri. *Blues People. Negro Music in White America.* New York: William Morrow and Company, 1963, p. I.

· 33. Ibid., p. 4.

34. Courlander, Harold. *Afro-American Folklore.* New York: G. Schirmer, 1914, p. 73.

35. Courlander, Harold. *The Drum and the Hoe. Life and Lore of the Haitian People.* Berkeley: University of California Press, 1960, p. 127.

36. Lomax, p. 64.

Chapter 2

1. Sowande, Fela. *The Role of Music in African Society.* Washington D.C.: Howard University Press, 1969, p. 27.

2. Ventura, Michael. *Shadow Dancing in the USA.* Los Angeles: Jeremy P. Tarcher, Inc., 1985, p. 112.

3. Quoted in Charters, Samuel. *The Roots of the Blues: An African Search.* New York: G.P. Putnam's Sons, 1981, p. i.

4. From the introduction by David Ames. *Wolof Music of Senegal and Gambia.* Ethnic Folkways Library Album # FE4462 New York: Folkways Record and Service Corp., 1955.

5. Lomax, Alan. *The Land Where the Blues Began.* New York: Pantheon Books, 1993, p. 356.

6. From the introduction by David Ames. *Wolof Music of Senegal and Gambia.* Ethnic Folkways Library Album # FE4462 New York: Folkways Record and Service Corp., 1955.

7. Burr-Reynaud, Frederic. *Anathemes.* Port-au-Prince: La Press, 1930, p. 190.

8. Quoted in Palmer, Robert. *Rock & Roll: an unruly history.* New York: Harmony Books, 1995, p. 15.

9. Roberts, John Storm. *Black Music of Two Worlds.* Tivoli: Original Music, 1972, p. 33.

10. Baraka, Amiri. *Blues People. Negro Music in White America.* New York: William Morrow and Company, 1963, p. 41.

11. Oliver, Paul. *Savannah Syncopators. African Retentions in the Blues.* New York: Stein and Day, 1970, p. 76.

12. Palmer, p. 31.

13. Oliver, p. 73.

14. Ibid., p. 56-7.

15. Ibid., p. 76.

16. Palmer, Robert. *Deep Blues.* New York: The Viking Press, 1981, p. 27.

17. Schuller, Gunther, quoted in Oliver, p. 14.

18. Oliver, p. 61.

19. Sonnier, Austin. *A Guide to the Blues: History, Who's Who, Resources.* Westport, CT: Greenwood Press, 1994, pp. 6-7.

20. Roberts, p. 3.

21. Lomax, p. 356.

Chapter 3

1. "Play" Lee Lozowick and Ed Flaherty. Copyright 1997. Used by permission.

2. "Driftin'" Lee Lozowick and Ed Flaherty. Copyright 1997. Used by permission.

3. Lomax, Alan. *The Land Where the Blues Began.* New York: Pantheon Books, 1993, p. 63.

4. Ibid., p. 58.

5. Wilcock, Donald E., with Buddy Guy. *Damn Right I've Got the Blues: Buddy Guy and the Blues Roots of Rock & Roll.* San Francisco: Woodward Press, 1993, p. 11.

6. Epstein, Dena. *Sinful Tunes and Spirituals.* Chicago: University of Chicago Press, 1977, p. 201.

7. Cone, Stephen R. *The Spirituals and the Blues.* Maryknoll: Orbis Books, 1972, p. 183.

8. Quoted in Lomax, p. 63.

9. Eliade, Mircea, Editor in Chief. *Encyclopedia of Religions.* New York: MacMillan Publishing Co., 1987, p. 63.

10. Lomax, p. 18.

11. House, Eddie. "Preachin' the Blues" Used by permission.

12. McDowell, Fred. Quoted in Welding, Pete. "Fred McDowell Talking," in *Nothing but the Blues.* Mike Leadbitter, Editor, London, Spring, 1971, p.146.

13. Lomax, p. 355.

14. From a conversation with the author, Feb. 21, 1998.

Chapter 4

1. James, Elmore. "My Bleeding Heart." Used by permission.

2. Dubois, W.E.B. *The Souls of Black Folk.* Quoted in: Finn, Julio. *The Bluesman: the Musical Heritage of Black Men and Women in the Americas.* London: Quartet Books, 1986, p. 5.

3. Quoted in Taylor, Rogan P. *The Death and Resurrection Show: from Shaman to Superstar.* London: Anthony Blond, 1985, p. 57.

4. Nadel, Siegfried. Quoted in Nettl, Bruno. *The Role of Music in Primitive Culture.* Cambridge: Harvard University Press, 1956, p. 7.

5. Senghor, Leopold. Quoted in Kestleoot, Lilyan. *Black Writers in French: A Literary History of Negritude Philosophy.* Temple University Press, 1974, p. 87.

6. Quoted in McKee, Margaret and Fred Chisenhall, *Beale, Black and Blue: Life and Music on Black America's Main Street.* Baton Rouge: Louisiana State University Press, 1981, p. 170.

7. Sachs, Curt. *Our Musical Heritage: A Short History of Music.* Englewood Cliffs: Prentice Hall Inc., 1948, p. 3.

8. Lomax, Alan. *The Land Where the Blues Began.* New York: Pantheon Books, 1993, p. 70.

9. Taylor, p. 11.

10. Quoted in Palmer, p.46.

11. Taylor, Koko. "I'm a Woman." Used by permission.

12. Roberts, John Storm. *Black Music of Two Worlds.* Tivoli: Original Music, 1972, p. 33.

13. Quoted in Trynka, Paul. *Portrait of the Blues.* New York: Da Capo Press, 1996, p. 148

14. Quoted in Ibid., p. 153.
15. Quoted in Ibid., p. 21.
16. Quoted in Guralnick, Peter. *Searching for Robert Johnson.* New York: E.P. Dutton, 1982, p. 18.
17. Palmer, p. 60.

Chapter 5

1. Quoted in Serrano, Juan and Jose Elgorriaga. *Flamenco, Body and Soul. An Aficionado's Introduction.* Fresno: The Press at California State University, 1990, p. vii.
2. Ibid., p. 117.
3. Leblon, Bernard. *Gypsies and Flamenco. The emergence of the art of flamenco in Andalusia.* Hatfield, England: University of Hertfordshire Press, 1995, p. 14.
4. Lomax, Alan and Eduardo Torner. Liner notes to *The Columbia World Library of Folk and Primitive Music—Vol. 14: Spanish Folk Music.* Compiled and Edited by Alan Lomax.
5. Dawanellos, Nick. "Les Tsiganes et la Musique Grecque." in *Tsiganes: Identité, Evolution.* Paris: Etudes, Tsiganes Syros Alternatives, 1989, pp. 489-95.
6. Alimatov, Turgun. Quoted in Levin, Theodore. *The Hundred Thousand Fools of God: Musical Travels in Central Asia (and Queens, New York).* Bloomington: Indiana University Press, 1996, p. 102.
7. Serrano, p. 80.
8. Unpublished lyric. Quoted in Hecht, Paul. *The Wind Cried. An American's Discovery of the World of Flamenco.* New York: The Dial Press, Inc., 1968, p. 70.
9. Starkie, Walter, Litt.D. *Don Gypsy: Adventures with a Fiddle in Southern Spain.* New York: E.P. Dutton and Company, Inc., 1937, p. 65.
10. Leblon, p. 99.
11. Lorca, Frederico Garcia. *Poet in New York.* New York: Grove Press, 1955, pp.156-162.
12. Quoted in Serrano, p. 58.
13. Pena, Pedro. Quoted in Serrano, p.72.
14. Charters, Samuel. *The Roots of the Blues: An African Search.* New York: G.P. Putnam's Sons, 1981, p. 125.
15. Reymond, Lizelle and Sri Anirvan. *To Live Within: Teachings of a Baul.* High Burton: Coombe Springs Press, 1984, p. 243.
16. Quoted in Tawagoto, Fall 1991, Volume 4, Number 4, p.8.

17. Khan, Hazrat Inayat, *The Mysticism of Sound and Music. A Sufi Message of Spiritual Liberty, Vol. II* (revised). Geneva: The International HeadQuarters of the Sufi Movement, 1991, p. 2.

18. Quoted in Bhattacharya, Bhaskar. *The Path of the Mystic Lover: Baul Songs of Passion and Ecstasy.* Rochester: Destiny Books, 1993, p. 27.

19. Sarkar, R.M. *Bauls of Bengal: In Quest of the Man of the Heart.* New Delhi: Gian Publishing House, 1990, p. 161.

20. Bhattacharya, p. 24.

21. Sen, Kshitimohan. *Medieval Mysticism of India.* (translated from the Bengali by Manomohan Ghosh) New Delhi: Oriental Books Reprint Collection, 1974, p. 202.

22. Palmer, Robert. *Rock & Roll: an unruly history.* New York: Harmony Books, 1995, p. 124.

23. Lozowick, Lee and Ed Flaherty. "Blind Devotion."Copyright 1995. Used by permission.

Chapter 6

1. Quoted in Lomax, Alan. *The Land Where the Blues Began.* New York: Pantheon Books, 1993, p. 305.

2. Quoted in Neff, Robert and Anthony Connor. *Blues.* Boston: David R. Godine, Publisher, 1975, p. 1.

3. Nietzche, Friedrich. *Beyond Good and Evil: Prelude to a Philosophy of the Future,* (Translated by Walter Kauffman). New York: Vintage, 1989, p. 1.

4. Lozowick, Lee and Ed Flaherty. "Don't Make Promises." Copyright 1996. Used by permission.

5. Quoted in *Rock & Roll* © 1995 WGBH Educational Foundation and the BBC. David Espar, senior producer. South Burlington, VT: WGBH, 1995.

6. Quoted in Bane, Michael. *White Boy Singin' the Blues: The Black Roots of White Rock.* New York: Da Capo Press, 1982, p. 115.

7. Charters, Samuel. *The Country Blues.* New York: Da Capo Press, 1959, p. 241.

8. Palmer, Robert. *Rock & Roll: an unruly history.* New York: Harmony Books, 1995, p. 46.

9. Ibid., p. 46.

10. Quoted in Hart, Mickey. *Drumming at the Edge of Magic: A Journey into the Spirit of Percussion.* San Francisco: Harper Collins, 1990, p. 195.

11. Ventura, Michael. *Shadow Dancing in the USA.* Los Angeles: Jeremy P. Tarcher, Inc., 1985, p. 141.

12. Mander, Jerry. *In the Absence of the Sacred: The Failure of Technology and the Survival of the Indian Nations.* San Francisco: Sierra Club Books, 1991, p. 31.

13. Lomax, Alan. Quoted in an interview with Arnold Rypens, in *Back to the Roots* #14 May, 1997, p. 33.

14. Gomelsky, Giorgio. Quoted in Palmer, p. 113.

15. Ventura, p. 48.

16. Bane, p. 190.

17. Kerouac, Jack. *On the Road.* London: The Penguin Group, 1988, pp. 169-170.

18. Simic, Charles. "No Cure for the Blues," in *Antaeus: On Music.* No. 71/72, Autumn, 1993. Ed. by Daniel Halpern. p. 138.

19. Lozowick, Lee and Ed Flaherty. "Blues School." Copyright 1996. Used by permission.

20. Quoted in Bane, p. 135.

Chapter 7

1. Simic, Charles. "No Cure for the Blues," in *Antaeus: On Music.* No. 71/72, Autumn, 1993. Ed. by Daniel Halpern, p. 135.

2. Cone, Stephen R. *The Spirituals and the Blues.* Maryknoll: Orbis Books, 1972, p. 114.

3. Levine, Lawrence W. *Black Culture and Black Consciousness.* New York: Oxford University Press, 1977, p. 273.

4. Mezzrow, Milton. Quoted in Keil, Charles. *Urban Blues.* Chicago: University of Chicago Press, 1966, p. 99.

5. Lozowick, Lee and Ed Flaherty. "The Great Equalizer." Copyright 1998. Used by permission.

6. Lozowick, Lee and Ed Flaherty. "Earthly Love." Copyright 1997. Used by permission.

7. Jong, Erica. *The Devil at Large.* New York: Random House, 1993, p. 112.

8. Lozowick, Lee and Ed Flaherty. "Hooked by Your Eyes." Copyright 1996. Used by permission.

Endnotes

Selected Bibliography

I read scores of books for this project, but I list here only a few of my favorites. I want to make special mention of Alan Lomax's work, *The Land Where the Blues Began*. If you read only one book on the blues, read this one. I wish this book were on the reading list of every high school in the nation, because it is a piece of our history everyone needs to hear.

Bane, Michael. *White Boy Singin' the Blues: The Black Roots of White Rock.* New York: Da Capo Press, 1982.

Baraka, Amiri. *Blues People. Negro Music in White America.* New York: William Morrow and Company, 1963.

Bhattacharya, Deben. *Songs of the Bards of Bengal.* New York: Grove Press, Inc., 1969.

Bebey, Francis. *African Music. A People's Art.* New York: Lawrence Hilland Company, 1975.

Carruth, Hayden. *Sitting In: Selected Writings on Jazz, Blues and Related Topics.* Iowa City: University of Iowa Press, 1993.

Charters, Samuel. *The Legacy of the Blues. A glimpse into the art and lives of twelve great bluesmen. An informal study.* London: Calder & Boyers, 1975.

Charters, Samuel. *The Roots of the Blues: An African Search.* New York: G.P. Putnam's Sons, 1981.

Chernoff, John Miller. *African Rhythm and African Sensibility.* Chicago: University of Chicago Press, 1979.

Cone, Stephen R. *The Spirituals and the Blues.* Maryknoll: Orbis Books, 1972.

Dalton, David. *Piece of My Heart: The Life, Times and Legend of Janis Joplin.* New York: St. Martin's Press, 1971.

Deren, Maya. *Divine Horsemen. The Living Gods of Haiti.* New Paltz: McPherson and Company, 1953.

Finn, Julio. *The Bluesman: the Musical Heritage of Black Men and Women in the Americas.* London: Quartet Books, 1986.

Guralnick, Peter. *Searching for Robert Johnson.* New York: E.P. Dutton, 1982.

Hecht, Paul. *The Wind Cried. An American's Discovery of the World of Flamenco.* New York: The Dial Press, Inc., 1968.

Leblon, Bernard. *Gypsies and Flamenco. The emergence of the art of flamenco in Andalusia.* Hatfield: University of Hertfordshire Press, 1995.

Levin, Theodore. *The Hundred Thousand Fools of God: Musical Travels in Central Asia (and Queens, New York)*. Bloomington: Indiana University Press, 1996.

Lomax, Alan. *The Land Where the Blues Began*. New York: Pantheon Books, 1993.

Murray, Charles Shaar. *Crosstown Traffic: Jimi Hendrix and the Rock 'n' Roll Revolution*. New York: St. Martin's Press, 1989.

Neff, Robert and Anthony Connor. *Blues*. Boston: David R. Godine, Publisher, 1975.

Obrecht, Jas, Editor. *Blues Guitar: the Men who Made the Music*. From the pages of *Guitar Player* magazine. San Francisco: GPI Books, 1990.

Oliver, Paul. *Conversation with the Blues*. London: Cassell, 1965.

Oliver, Paul. *The Story of the Blues*. London: Barrie & Rockliff. The Cresset Press, 1969.

Oliver, Paul. *Savannah Syncopators. African Retentions in the Blues*. New York: Stein and Day, 1970.

Palmer, Robert. *Deep Blues*. New York: The Viking Press, 1981.

Palmer, Robert. *Rock & Roll: an unruly history*. New York: Harmony Books, 1995.

Roberts, John Storm. *Black Music of Two Worlds*. Tivoli: Original Music, 1972.

Sackheim, Eric. *The Blues Line: A Collection of Blues Lyrics*. New York: Grossman Publishers, Inc., 1969.

Serrano, Juan and Jose Elgorriaga . *Flamenco, Body and Soul. An Aficionado's Introduction*. Fresno: The Press at California State University, 1990.

Spencer, Jon Michael. *Re-Searching Black Music*. Knoxville: The University of Tennessee Press, 1996.

Taylor, Rogan P. *The Death and Resurrection Show: from Shaman to Superstar*. London: Anthony Blond, 1985.

Ventura, Michael. *Shadow Dancing in the USA*. Los Angeles: Jeremy P. Tarcher, Inc., 1985.

Text Credits

Every effort has been made to trace copyright holders of the material in this book. The editor apologizes if any work has been used without permission and would be glad to be told of anyone who has not been consulted.

Excerpts from "Blues" by Robert Neff and Anthony Conner, published by David R. Godine. Used with permission of IMG Bach Agency.

Excerpts from "Love Song of the Dark Lord," by Barbara Stoller Miller. Copyright © 1977, Columbia University Press. Reprinted with permission of the publisher.

Excerpt from "The Wind Cried: An American's Discovery of the World of Flamenco" by Paul Hecht, © 1968. Doubleday, a division of Bantam Doubleday Dell Publishing Group, Inc. Used with permission of the publisher.

Excerpt from "Flamenco, Body and Soul" by Jose Seranno, © 1990. The Press at California State University, Fresno, Calif. Used with permission of the publisher.

Lyrics Credits

"I Be's Troubled." Written by Muddy Waters. ©1959, 1987 Watertoons Music (BMI)/Administered by Bug Music. All Rights Reserved. Used by permission.

"Preachin' Blues." Written by Son House. ©Renewed 1997 Sondick Music (BMI)/Administered by Bug Music. All Rights Reserved. Used by permission.

"I'm a Woman" by Ellas McDaniel and Koko Taylor. (© 1955 Renewed), 1957 Arc Music Corporation. All Rights Reserved. Used by Permission. International Copyright Secured.

"Five Long Years" by Eddie Boyd. Copyright © 1952 (Renewed) Embassy Music Corp. (BMI). All Rights Reserved. Used by permission.

"My Bleeding Heart." Written by Elmore James and Marshall Seehorn. All attempts to trace the copyright holder for this material have proved unsuccessful.

"My Black Mama." Written by Son House. All attempts to trace the copyright holder for this material have proved unsuccessful.

"Urban Voodoo Juice." Written by Salome Arnold. All attempts to trace the copyright holder for this material have proved unsuccessful.

About the Author

Ed Flaherty was born in New York City in 1968. He fled to Arizona in 1989 to Prescott, Arizona, where he completed a degree in psychology and religious studies. When Ed's not on the road with Shri, he makes his living blowing glass for a small local company. Playing the guitar has been a constant in his life since the age of eleven, but, since joining Shri in 1993, music has become an obsession. He plans to continue studying the musical traditions of the world, and describing the relationship between the religious and musical life of human beings.

RETAIL ORDER FORM

Name _____ Phone ( ) _____

Street Address or P.O. Box _____

City _____ State _____ Zip Code _____

	QTY	ITEM	ITEM PRICE	TOTAL PRICE	
1		GOOD THING. AUDIOCASSETTE	$10.00		
2		MIZ BLUES SHOOZ. AUDIOCASSETTE	$10.00		
3		MIZ BLUES SHOOZ. CD	$15.00		
4		HOOKED. AUDIOCASSETTE	$10.00		
5		HOOKED. CD	$15.00		
6		SHRISON IN HELL. AUDIOCASSETTE	$10.00		
7		SHRISON IN HELL. CD	$15.00		
8		T-SHIRTS. S-M-L-XL-XXL — ALL SIZES	$15.00		
9		BASEBALL CAPS	$10.00		
10		THE BLUES ALIVE	$16.95		
			SUBTOTAL:		
			SHIPPING: (see below)		
			TOTAL:		

- FOR U.S. ORDERS
  ADD $1.00 FOR FIRST ITEM FOR SHIPPING
  ADD .50¢ FOR EACH ADDITIONAL ITEM FOR SHIPPING

- FOR FOREIGN ORDERS
  ADD 25% OF SUBTOTAL FOR SHIPPING

MAKE CHECK PAYABLE IN U.S. FUNDS ONLY TO:
BAD POET PRODUCTIONS
P.O. BOX 4272
PRESCOTT, AZ 86302
TEL: (520) 778-9189
FAX: (520) 717-1779